God, Mystery, and Mystification

GOD
MYSTERY &
MYSTIFICATION

Denys Turner

UNIVERSITY OF NOTRE DAME PRESS

NOTRE DAME, INDIANA

University of Notre Dame Press
Notre Dame, Indiana 46556
www.undpress.nd.edu

Copyright © 2019 by the University of Notre Dame

Published in the United States of America

Library of Congress Control Number: 2019948599

ISBN: 978-0-268-10597-6 (Hardback)
ISBN: 978-0-268-10600-3 (WebPDF)
ISBN: 978-0-268-10599-0 (Epub)

For Courtney

CONTENTS

PREFACE

At a farewell reception upon my leaving Cambridge University for Yale, my colleague and friend Douglas Hedley said that I had "no school." Until he said it I had never thought of it, but once he said it I saw it was true, and I rather took a fancy to the thought—as I took it that Douglas intended I should. It goes together with there being something positive about lacking a school that, as a lifelong academic, I have thought of myself as primarily a teacher of students, not a writer of books, and a teacher seeks no following, aiming rather to liberate students so that they can choose their own way—indeed, it is your job as a teacher to cast them off at the first sign of attachment.

It has seemed to me that as a practice teaching differs from a form of self-congratulatory propaganda on behalf of one's own insights in that the true teacher disappears into the act of teaching itself, so that you see and attend to the matter taught, not the teacher. Such a disposition is not easy to acquire and harder to sustain. It demands of you the sort of disappearing act that you quickly discern at work in the writing of that most selfless of all teachers, Thomas Aquinas. Of course he has a style of his own, though paradoxically that style seems designed to the end of keeping himself out of the picture—what is distinctive about Thomas is that he doesn't stand out. And in that paradoxical conjunction it would also seem that he aspired to reflect the image of his maker: for, as another Dominican teacher, Meister Eckhart, said, God is distinct from everything else whatsoever in that God is the one being who is not-distinct; or as Nicholas of Cusa put it, in any of the ways in which we distinguish one creature from another, God is the one and only *non-aliud*, "not-other"—and so God uniquely is able to be one with us all. Because of this, Bonaventure, briefly Thomas's colleague at the University of Paris, said that God is the

ix

ultimate disappearing act, "truly . . . a hidden God"; for God is like the
light in which we see, pervading the whole world and making it present to
us in all its richness of color on condition that it is itself invisible in not
being another object of sight. For the university teacher to have a school
seems to me to be troublingly close to imposing a personal presence upon
the taught; it is to become a sight to be seen, and so it is to fail to provide
the light in which to see.

Brought together in this volume are some secondary written by-
products of that primarily oral teaching practice. They are here in print, of
course, but even in this form I have tried to communicate in a style as near
as possible to how teachers do it in the lecture. That said, it is alas time now
to admit that in one crucial matter it is evident that I need to gloss my own
work, for in this connection, if in no other, I have failed satisfactorily to
communicate. Perhaps as a result of a certain looseness of terminology or
argument on my part, perhaps in consequence of some less than full attention on the part of some readers (it is really not for me to say which accounts for it), some of my published works have unintentionally caused it
to be thought that when I speak favorably of a general metatheological
doctrine of "negative theology," it is as if to claim some epistemic priority
for negative forms of theological speech over affirmative.

I do not think any such thing. I have never thought it. I have never intentionally taught or written it, nothing in the essays here presented sup-
ports such a view, and I am happy to disown any statement implying it that
in the past might accidentally have found its way into what I have written
or said. With what tedious frequency have I cited Aristotle's dictum, as
Thomas Aquinas knew of it in Latin translation, *eadem est scientia oppositorum*, which is to say that affirmations and their corresponding negations
are inseparable and of equal logical and semantic standing. For that reason, if the nature of God is to be beyond all affirmations then equally failing of God must be our negations. It certainly cannot be that negations get
a firm hold on God where the grip of affirmation slips, as Thomas Aquinas,
in an uncharacteristic lapse of accurate interpretation, mistakenly seems to
have thought the great Jewish philosopher Maimonides maintained. What
falls short of God is language, the whole cathedral of speech, formed at
once of presenting mass and absenting space, neither of affirming mass
without the space it encloses, nor of negating space without the enclosing

mass—for without both at once there is no shape, no architecture; and it is only in the distinctive form of their conjunction that we possess the transcending mystery of Cuthbert's place in Durham or Abbot Suger's at St. Denis in Paris. Some generalized prioritization of the theologically negative over the theologically affirmative misses the point entirely; and as there can be no architecture on such terms, so there cannot be theology without that conjunction. I have never defended so vacuous a doctrine of the negative as somehow theologically prior, and if for no other reason, then for the reason that Duns Scotus gives, reacting, it would seem, to some thoughtlessly apophatic zealotries of his time: *negationes [etiam] non summe amamus*, he says, or as one might paraphrase, it's not negations that we love in the highest degree.

So much is what I have always said, and I think clearly enough except perhaps once in the last chapter of a book I wrote years ago called *The Darkness of God*. There, in the articulation of this complex intertwining of the positive and the negative, I may have unintentionally caused some confusion among readers: for I seem to have said that as within our speech about God there are elements of grammatical affirmation and negation, often conjoint—as when we say affirmatively that God is "wise" and in the same breath also negatively that God is "infinitely" so—so also is there a second-order failure, a negation, I said, of speech as such. And this second level of negation supervenes upon the first so as to indicate the failure of the conjunction of grammatical affirmation and negation. Putting the matter that way was indeed unhelpful, for it did seem to assign to this second moment of theological transcendence some precedence of the theologically negative as to the last word—though I never meant that at all. And though I said I didn't mean that (especially in that last chapter of *The Darkness of God*) it did nonetheless sound to some ears as if I was saying that in the end the negations trump the affirmations. I was wrong to give that impression, and it was my fault. Why I did not say more simply what I meant, namely that beyond the articulation of the affirmative and negative ways is the way of what Thomas called "eminence," which yields neither to the affirmative nor to the negative, being, in a sense that is quite beyond us, quite beyond us—that I cannot now say. For when all is said and done, it is not some crowning negation any more than it is some curious form of superaffirmation that we are left with: what's there at the end, and there "eminently," is simply a sort of stunned silence before God in that place in the soul where it is at last at prayer.

Wonderful then is the variety of ways in which medieval theologians have differently worked through that transcendence of theological speech that is its final achievement, in the interplay between the language that affirms and the language that denies, and in the demonstration that even the complex conjunction, having in the meantime done its theological work, in ultimately failing of resolution opens up the space of the contemplative. Over now five decades I have had the opportunity to observe that complexity of speech as it has been played out in one way by Augustine, in another by the pseudo-Denys, and in countless variations of the Augustinian and Dionysian styles in Gregory the Great, Bernard of Clairvaux, Thomas Aquinas, Bonaventure, Marguerite Porete and Meister Eckhart, Jan van Ruusbroec, the *Cloud* author, Julian of Norwich, Denys the Carthusian, and John of the Cross. Whenever I wrote of them I found them saying what in his own very different way Wittgenstein also said, that there is no capturing the foundations of language within language itself, though here too I have always resisted the empiricist injunction of his *Tractatus* that because "one cannot speak thereof" only silence is permissible. For though it is true that before the mystery of God there is no getting hold by means of language of that which inherently exceeds its reach, nonetheless there is a way of gesturing toward that failure-that-is-also-eminence indirectly in a strategy, deployed perhaps most tellingly within my company of medieval theologians by Julian of Norwich, by way not of the minimization of linguistic resources but of their exuberant proliferation. Julian's deployment of a rich theological vocabulary, strategically piling up image upon conflicting image—typically she tells us of her "holy mother Jesus" that "he" speaks to us—so press upon the limits of speech that, being thus hopelessly overburdened, speech itself collapses into unknowing simply under the weight of its affirmative excess.

All my theologians tell of this in one way or another, and I engage in the second part of this collection with some late medieval controversies about how exactly to construct that relationship between mystical speech and its failure-in-transcendence, though there is material also in the first part that looks forward to that central, defining feature of Christian faith's articulated inarticulacy, to what Nicholas of Cusa called a *docta ignorantia*—which means simply that you have to work hard at a refined discipline of unknowing to be cut out for the theological task, for you do not enter the mystery of God simply by throwing in the theological towel. The Spirit's dove, as Gerard Manley Hopkins says, "comes with work to do." And as I say in the third of these papers, the theologians who sweat over these second-order questions have their correlates among the poets and the musicians; they do it better, they perspire over it less, theirs is a less defensive palaver than that of the theologians, and they do it more as a matter of course. If the professional theologians theoretically say it, the poets practically show it, and that is why Hopkins in one way, George Herbert in another, and supremely Dante in a third are among my favorite demotic theological writers. And not one of them is a negative theologian, though all three are, I suppose, mystics; and on the matter of what that much-abused word means, why not let the poets have the first say—for my part it was on their account, especially because of Hopkins, that I ever had any thoughts about it.

Scattered as the thoughts are in this miscellany, I did hope when assembling them to identify at least some consistency there, if not something more, something or other positive that they add up to. In one way or another they are all about the mystery of God and about how to tell it apart from merely idolatrous mystifications. Specifically a loosely connected set of essays in the first part of this volume occupy some thematic common ground in addressing issues of theological language in a general and theoretical manner; and it might seem hard to connect them with those of the last essay on the political dimension of the theology of Herbert McCabe. And I must admit that I do not have in those essays any formal methodological prescriptions to offer governing connections between abstractly speculative and concretely practical forms of theology, nor was I inclined when assembling this collection to attempt any such thing.

For they do connect, and the third of these essays says something about why. I am not sure that I need a theory of how they do it because I cannot see how you could keep apart accounts of what you can say in theological speculation from what you must say politically otherwise than in a contrived disjunction inserted into the narrative of Jesus's life and death as it is told in the Gospel accounts. Jesus's prayers of dereliction in the Garden of Gethsemane and on the cross at Calvary connect with Herbert's

political theology insofar as the death of Jesus was itself an overtly political event—not, I should say, intentionally so, as if Jesus had some political
theology or program to offer, just inevitably so short of dogmatically in-
serting some theological option resistant to such politics—and that would
be a political ploy anyway, since if you understand anything about politics
you know you say something political in the very act of attempting to get
away from it. You don't have to invent a discrete curricular space for a discipline of "political theology." You just have to resist the forms of abstraction that purport to keep politics and theology apart, for the disjunctions
imposed by some between religion and politics are themselves, obviously,
political in their consequences when they are not (as is more often the
case) politically motivated in the first place. Herbert put the connection
with characteristic simplicity: "If you do not love you are scarcely alive. But
if you do love you will certainly be killed." Love is always a matter of life
and death, as the Song of Songs says.

In that essay on the darkness of God—it is for once not about our
darkened theological minds confronted with the depths of the divine,
but about Jesus's own darkened mind confronted with the death-dealing
depravities of the human—the formal, logically necessary, second-order
vocabulary of the divine transcendence beyond all speech is made a substantive reality in his person and most concretely, if also most alarmingly,
in his death on the cross. Empty and merely pious platitude achieves no
grip on this: Jesus does not somehow or other mysteriously "die for our
sins." Our sins killed him, he was executed as a political subversive for the
usual reason that what he had to say was something we—the world—
could not afford to admit to. Given that truly he was incarnate, *perfectus
homo*, the whole meaning of the Incarnation entailed that he was given no
choice, even if, as *perfectus Deus*, he irrelevantly was beyond all freedoms
free. And if Jesus willingly submitted to death on the cross, eschewing a
pointless armed resistance, he was nonetheless bowing to the inevitable as
a sinful world and its attendant politics have constructed these matters. As
to all that, in the story's end it is clear, at any rate as Mark tells of it, that
Jesus himself did not know what to say about it, he too was lost for words
as to why, as it seemed, he was so utterly forsaken, even by his own Father.

St. Paul says that Jesus made no appeal to his divinity, whether before
the Sanhedrin or before Pilate, tempted as he was to do so in Gethsemane.

There, when he is pleading in prayer that it might not be, the synoptic evangelists show what was the price of his restraint. His was a mission achieved in the only way possible, that is, by way of its collapsing around his ears. For had Jesus pulled off a victory it would have been on the world's terms that he had done so. The one way in which he could have failed to open up a real alternative to that of his oppressors was by successfully challenging their power on their terms; and that refusal of their politics *is* politics, whether you like to admit it or not. Nietzsche says sarcastically what Paul joyfully asseverates, that victory by way of weakness, vulnerability, and failure was the only option for Jesus; it was as armed with powerlessness that he challenged his oppressors, with his being forsaken by his Father and his not knowing why.

Here then is the darkness of God made incarnate in the politically motivated execution of an innocent man. The rest of what is contained in this volume, in that methodological first part and the medieval focus of the second, is just tinkering with the theological epistemology consequent upon that execution. I don't always know how to make that connection between the epistemology and the politics in a formal and theoretical way. It takes some of us an inordinate amount of time, unnecessarily extended perhaps by a philosopher's excessive attention to the second-order, to get to the point that the centurion standing by the cross seems to have grasped upon hardly a moment's notice, that here in this politically motivated execution of an innocent man was all the meaning of God: find it there or not at all.

In any case there it is. If it is only rather late in the day and laboriously by way of the Areopagus in Athens, it goes to show that even a philosopher can eventually make it to Good Friday in Jerusalem.

Denys Turner

ACKNOWLEDGMENTS

The papers in this collection are previously unpublished with the exception of the third, which in an earlier version, here heavily revised, was published in *Redeeming Truth, Considering Faith and Reason*, ed. Laurence Paul Hemming and Susan Frank Parsons (London: SCM Press, 2007), 15–33, and the last, on the theology of Herbert McCabe, in this case only a little revised. It was first delivered to an audience at the Dominican House of Studies, Blackfriars, Oxford, in partial celebration of the eight-hundredth anniversary of the founding of the Order of Preachers and was then published in *New Blackfriars* in November 2016. All the rest were talks given over some thirty years or more to student groups and faculty and on occasions of different kinds, as follows. Chapter 1 was a paper delivered in its original form to the Catholic Society at Harvard University in the fall of 2016, and then in a revised form at a graduate seminar of the Lumen Christi Institute in Columbia University in January 2017; chapter 2 was a public lecture delivered in August 2016 within the research program on atheism of the Australian Catholic University in Melbourne; chapter 4 was a paper read at a seminar on metaphors of the erotic in world religions at New York University sometime in the 1980s; chapter 5 was in an earlier draft a paper I read to graduate students of history at a seminar in Christ Church College Oxford, as I recall sometime in the 1990s, though it was the work of Rebecca Stephens in her fine doctoral dissertation at the University of Birmingham, "Orthodoxy and Liminality in Marguerite Porete's *Mirror of Simple Souls*," that inspired me to write about Marguerite in the way that I did; chapter 6 was a paper read to a seminar in Heythrop College in the University of London in the 1990s on love in world religions; and chapter 7 was an introductory lecture for the opening of a conference entitled "Why Is There Anything?" assembling a

varied collection of cosmologists, philosophers, and theologians in October 2011 at Yale University. Most of these papers I have revised for publi-
cation, but only very lightly, leaving them almost word for word as they
were delivered, and as a result there are some small overlaps and a few
brief repetitions, especially between the fifth and the sixth, that I have not
attempted to edit out. Also, having originated as talks they were spoken to
the ear, not written in print form for the eye, which may account for some
remaining peculiarities of style that even my skilled and sensitive copy editor at the University of Notre Dame Press, Elisabeth Magnus, was unable
to persuade me to edit out.

In the fifty years or so of my academic career I have accumulated
many intellectual debts, most immediately to two careful readers for the
Notre Dame University Press, William Franke and David Burrell, one a new
friend and the other one of my oldest. I assembled this collection within the
time frame of my tenure of a research fellowship at the Australian Catholic University, and as a contribution to its program on atheism, and I am
grateful for the university's financial support, but more especially for the
fellowship and friendship of that excellent team of researchers, headed by
David Newheiser and Robyn Horner.

Two others are owed incalculable debts of intellectual and moral
friendship for almost the whole length of my academic career. What I owe
to the late Herbert McCabe is bound to be greater than I know, though I
do know it to have been profound and pervasive. Anyone who knows his
work will upon reading several of the essays in this volume readily observe the depth and extent of his influence. And as long as I have known
Herbert's work I have known Terry Eagleton's. Along with Herbert it has
been Terry who has shown me how to bring together the theological and
political with clarity and wit—I think for the first time at a meeting of the
Pax Romana student society in University College Dublin in 1966, and
then on so many occasions thereafter. And he still continues to show it.

But the third debt is the greatest of all, that is, to my best friend, conversation partner, editor, indexer, critic, and wife, Courtney Palmbush. She
is to me, as Spinoza put it, *natura naturans* to my *natura naturata*. As without her my work in recent years would have been greatly diminished, and
with her it is as greatly inspired, so it is to her that I dedicate this book in
gratitude and love.

PART I

_____

MYSTERY

How Could a Good God Allow Evil?

WHERE TO START?

You are in Princeton and ask your way to Harvard. "If I were you," un-helpfully you are told, "I wouldn't start from here." Of course Harvard people might take a dim view of starting any journey from Princeton, least of all a journey to Harvard, for Harvard is the center of the universe and everyone knows that sensible journeys start from there. But if Prince-ton is where you are you don't have the choice, you have to start from there willy-nilly. And so it is with many problems, particularly those of a philosophical sort. In discussions about God and evil in our times it can seem obvious that the starting point must be with the question "How could a good God allow evil?" for it is as if the boot were on the skeptical foot; and it is as if it would be required of those who ask that question in hope of a theistic answer that they meet conditions of certainty and proof that in fact cannot be met. That is where the presumption seems to stand since Hume, whether in philosophical or literary treatments of the prob-lem of evil, whether in a John Stuart Mill or in a Dostoevsky.

Of course it is easy to see why the skeptical question is generally thought to be the better, if not the only, place to start. While for a person of any degree of sensitivity thoughts of the evil in our world may well present powerfully rational (and intensely emotional) reasons for doubting the existence of God, no one can reasonably doubt the existence of that evil. Hence it looks as if evil is a problem for belief in God in a way that belief in God can never as convincingly explain the world's evil, still less justify it. In the mid-eighteenth century David Hume put it that way round in what is perhaps the classical statement of the "problem of evil"— it's been where more or less everyone has started since. "Epicurus's old questions are yet unanswered," he says. "Is [God] willing to prevent evil, but not able? Then He is impotent. Is He able, but not willing? Then He is malevolent. Is He both able and willing? Whence then is evil?"[1]

You might, though, think that skepticism should be allowed to cut the other way too. For granted that there is no defense of theism that could demonstrate formal consistency between the evidence of the world's evils and belief in the power and goodness of God, there is an equally justified doubt whether an atheistic argument formally demonstrating inconsistency is the more conclusive. You can argue that Hume's questions are but that, questions, and that they may not be begged for all their undoubted force as rhetorical gestures. In a word, for all that Hume would have you conclude otherwise, his are in fact open questions. And if they are open then they deserve to be given a thoughtful answer, not a dismissive shrug of the shoulders. The question, then, is fair enough: If God is all good and almighty, whence evil? And were it to turn out that in truth it is impossible to settle that question one way or another, as it seems to Brian Davies, David Burrell, and Herbert McCabe among others, then while you don't have to conclude that Hume was wrong to ask the question, you do have to insist that he should not be allowed to get away with begging it.[2] It does after all matter where you start from.

And though there are arguments either way, given the prevailing Epicurean presumptions it seems preferable to start from Hume's skeptical question at least for a preliminary and dialectical purpose if not from a dogmatically atheist answer. For it does seem reasonable to concede that you have to start from the manifest and unchallengeable facts of evil, and if so it becomes the theist's job to show with convincing reasons why one might question the necessity of doing so. And just so as to anticipate where the argument will lead, at no point will I attempt to answer the

question of what would justify an all-good and all-powerful God's allowing evil of any kind to exist (at any rate directly), let alone allowing the extent of evil that there is; and that is because I take the view that we cannot
know the answer to that question one way or the other. In short, the matter is undecidable either way, that is, you can show that you couldn't know
the answer to it. And that is about as far as anyone, theist or atheist, can
get with the problem of evil. As to the question, then, "How could a good
God allow evil?" the only answer can be that it is impossible to say.

GOD AND NATURAL EVIL: HUME'S PROBLEM

When I say that we ought not to start by allowing Hume to beg the Epicurean question, because it is unanswerable either way, I do want to be
clear as to what I mean. Of course there is a problem of evil, if not necessarily expressed in Hume's form. But on anyone's account, not all evil is a
problem. Some evils we can take in our stride, there being no cause for
theological, philosophical or even moral alarm in them, and we should
start by taking the existence of such evils out of the debate. For example:
though others may have different convictions than I do about the matter,
I have personally never had a theological problem with lions eating an-
telopes,[3] though it is hard not to feel for the panicking beasts as they flee
their predators in such wonderfully graceful leaps and bounds; nor do I
find myself distressed that lions seem as unlikely as ever to get round to
lying down with lambs as Isaiah had hoped they would. For lions lying
down with lambs would be good news for lambs,[4] but it would be terrible
news for lions. It goes with being a lion that it eats lambs—being a lamb-
eating machine is built in to what a lion is. And more generally there seems
to be a rule here, nature requiring a level of raw indifference in matters of
tooth and claw: that is, if there is to be the variety and complexity of the
natural world at all and so that there be lions, alas, lambs are going to have
to pay for it with their lives. "Did he who made the lamb make thee?" asks
William Blake of the tiger burning bright, and it troubles him that the
Creator made both the savage and the savaged.[5] The question for him is
not rhetorical; but there really is no answer to Blake other than "Yes, God
did make tigers," and consistency requires of those who, like Blake, have a

problem of this kind that they consider what alternative world they have in mind that doesn't either replace a problem for lambs being eaten with a problem for carnivorous predators being starved for want of ovine nutrition, or desist from creating lions altogether and along with them all the obviously creatable predatory species.

It would appear to be the same with inanimate physical processes, for they sometimes have an impact unhappily, even tragically, upon human affairs. In the mid-eighteenth century an earthquake in Portugal killed thirty thousand and Voltaire lost faith in God. Rather more understandable would have been his loss of faith in human beings; it was they, after all, who built Lisbon on a geological fault line and seemed willing to blame any one or thing but their ignorance for the destructive outcome. We today have far less excuse for continuing to build a San Francisco on the San Andreas fault, and there seems to be something of a premodern and merely pagan superstition in supposing there would be a problem about God if some day soon San Francisco were to disappear forever down an immense sinkhole, for we do know now it is very likely that in due course it will.

And were it asked more generally why a good God who had alternatives available would create a world in which earthquakes are bound to happen, it is unclear what answer could meet the case. It would seem that in asking that sort of question about earthquakes we are asking about sets of physical processes the laws governing which originate at a point in time in the order of 13.799 ± 0.021 billion years ago. That is, to require God to have created only an earthquake-free world and to regret that he didn't is to regret too much, for to wish away earthquakes is to wish away the physical laws that govern the universe itself. There is no picking the good bits of physics from the bad, for that isn't physics at all. For if God makes a world in which there are predictable outcomes it is because God wants to create an intelligible world. But the world would become wholly incomprehensible to us if we could never know when physical laws were going to be suspended by God just to suit our particular preferences from time to time. Those physical laws exist precisely so that by getting to know them we can among other things learn to avoid building cities where we know that earthquakes are going to happen.

More challenging for some is the problem of physical pain. Hume, again, has taken the lead here. He seems to think it obvious that a world in which no one suffers physical pain would be a better world than the one we have got; and he asks why if God is good he should have chosen an alternative so obviously the worse of the two. "It seems . . . plainly possible," he says, "to carry on the business of life without any pain."[6] Hume's skeptical musings are rarely so thoughtless as when he speculates in this way, and there is a quick and sharp answer to him forthcoming from anyone suffering from that rare genetic disorder known as CIPA, the chronic inability to feel pain. Hume might be less convinced as to the advantages of a pain-free life had he given a moment's thought to the tragedy of a life threatened by scalding in overheated bath water that you cannot feel, by the prospect of limbs broken on which you walk unaware, of broken glass that you have trodden on in bare feet without noticing, or of a hand held in a flame from which there is no painful sensation to tell you of your limb's destruction. Then you might not be so easily convinced that bodily pain is altogether a bad thing, and you will hardly think you would be better off, taken in the round, for the want of it.

To which Hume, acknowledging that some pain has its purpose in animal life, nonetheless presses the point: Why so much pain, he asks, why unbearable pain?[7] Would not tolerable pain, or even some reduction in pleasure, serve the purpose of sending out the signals needed to warn of life-threatening courses of action, no purpose being served by intolerable pain? To which there is some sort of answer in the thought that pain cannot serve its purpose within the economy of human life if it occurs only at tolerable levels of mild discomfort. For, when tolerable, pain loses its point. Pain fails to do its job if it is less than too much, and still less effective is a simple reduction in one sort of pleasure relative to others. A cup of so-called "English" tea, in Harvard customarily emptied into the harbor in revulsion, has its pleasures of a sort that English people appreciate, if not Americans. Tea is not a painful drink just because it appears significantly to lack the thrills of Colombian coffee or of a fine red wine. Of course, it does not follow that we shouldn't try to reduce the levels of pain that visit us; but we should do so only to a safe extent, and a world in which analgesics were used to dull all pain to acceptable levels of discomfort would be a world in which, our bodies no longer serving with biological efficiency to warn us, we would have endlessly to calculate how to avoid physically harmful forms of behavior. Pain makes for an immensely more efficient warning device than sluggish brainpower with its turgidly inefficient capacity for truth and its ready aptness for self-deception.

None of these forms of evil, if indeed that is what they are, have any tendency to pose a problem of the kind that Hume thinks we are all forced to face. You can guarantee secure life for lambs only on condition of meek and mild vegetarian tigers and lions, or else none of them at all; you can have an earthquake-free cosmos only on condition that there are no reliable physical laws to govern it; you can have a world free of physical pain only if it is also a world free of physical pleasure, in short only if it is a world without nervous systems, and that is to say, a world without bodies. Given the kind of world that we have, these pains are necessary evils where they are not necessary goods,[8] in which case it is hard to see why the existence of them is to be regarded as providing rational evidence against God, since they seem just as plausibly to be arguments supportive of a providential benevolence within creation. In any case there is no need to bring God into the picture at this level at all, and it is no part of my argument that one should, since evolution will do as a perfectly good explanation for the emergence of the species that we have got, for the lions as for the lambs, and for why all animals have nervous systems that register pain with the intensity that they do. But if, like the pre-evolutionary Hume, and, in consort with some fundamentalist Christians of our time, you insist on bringing God into it one way or the other, the evidence from the natural world points at least as strongly against his atheist conclusion as in favor of it. Ours seems to be just the sort of natural world you might expect a good and wise God would bring about if God were to be bringing about any knowable form of natural world at all.

GOD AND MORAL EVIL: HUME'S PROBLEM

But as for moral evil, for evil done in the world, that would seem to be a very different matter. Here, at least, we might reasonably think that you have to start in Princeton, that is, with where we actually are, even if it would be better were we in Harvard where only good prevails. For here there really is a problem, and Hume half gets to it, if only in a sort of ironical throwaway to dismiss it; "Is [God] both able and willing" to prevent evil, he asks, and then rhetorically: "Whence then is evil?" It is here that we have to address how seriously that question should be taken. Hume is usually interpreted as simply begging the question in favor of a negative answer. On this account it seems that he cannot conceive of the possibility that the world we have, in which there is so much moral evil, might be exactly what an omnipotent and wholly good God should have willed, though in fact he shows nothing as to the inconsistency of maintaining both, he simply assumes it. And while Hume ought to have given more thought to his question and ought not be allowed just to shrug his shoulders as if the answer weighs too obviously against the existence of God, it does seem right to require not just Hume and the skeptics but also all theists to allow that there is a genuine problem here. "Whence then is evil?" is on all sides a real question, not a merely rhetorical one. And on all sides it should be admitted that even were a theistic answer unavailable to us in fact, there might still be an answer to it in principle, just so long as it is not a demonstrable contradiction to hold all three of Hume's propositions together, that God wills all good, that God is all powerful and can do all good, and that there is moral evil. I don't think Hume shows the conjunction to be inconsistent. But he does want to know what would show the conjunction to be consistent, and he doubts if any such demonstration is possible. In that at least I think he is right.

There is some reason, however, to step back from Hume and his eighteenth-century rationalist priorities, and from the general nondialectical strategy of seeking to ease the conceptual tension between the assertion of God and the pervasiveness of evil by means of the simple device of taking God out of the picture, leaving the evil unexplained beyond the assertion that it is par for the evolutionary (or some other) course. At least, Hume thought, removing God from the equation seemed intuitively to be a more satisfactory solution to the problem of evil than that of taking evil out of the picture, and, since Hume, the preponderance of opinion on both sides of the debate, theistic defenders and atheists alike, agrees with him that that is how the land lies. But in moving away from Hume I draw attention to a surprisingly different time, place, and style of reflection on the problem of evil, that of the fourteenth-century English theologian, Julian of Norwich, who shares one thing with Hume. Believing, unlike Hume, in the existence of a good and all-powerful God, she, like Hume, is quite baffled at the quandary thus caused by the quantity of sin that there is and at the viciousness of some of it. The difference between the medieval Julian and the modernist Hume is that Julian refuses to eliminate the problem, as Hume does, by dissolving it atheistically. But just as resolutely she refuses to dissolve it theologically; she confesses that she does not know for herself personally why a good and almighty God should create a world in which there is evil and that nothing in her understanding of Christian belief in a good and almighty God gives her an answer either. It might be thought surprising to advert to so unobvious a challenge to the worldly urbane Scottish skeptic as that of a medieval woman, one, it might be supposed, who is unlikely to outbid him whether for greater moral realism or for greater conceptual sophistication. Yet on both scores she is in fact the more complex and conceptually nuanced of the two.

GOD AND MORAL EVIL:
JULIAN OF NORWICH'S PROBLEM

Julian's book of her "shewings," as she calls them, is an extended set of meditations on a central problem, or set of problems, that personally beset her:[9] she is painfully troubled by her experience of evil and of that consciously evil human behavior that she calls, generically, "sin"—as who would not be who was alive and capable of reflection upon conditions in what must be the nastiest century, the fourteenth, in recorded Western history after our own recent twentieth,[10] ravaged as it was by interpersonal violence, disease, death, war, moral collapse, and economic decline. Julian herself, at the age of eight or nine, had survived a great plague, the so-called "Black Death," which in the space of two years took the lives of one-third of the population of England and of the European mainland. And in the face of her experience of the reality of evil of all kinds she is told in her showings that God does not see sin, that for God sin is "no thing," and that, contrary to all her own experience of evil, and especially of human sinfulness, "all will be well, and all will be well, and every manner of thing will be well."[11] So Julian is confronted with a dilemma: in view of the conjunction of her own intensely painful experience of sin (she says she experiences its presence in our world as a "sharp pain") and of the assurance that God does not admit to noticing it at all, she is compelled to seek some intellectual space within which the two conflicting propositions might be reconciled. You cannot sweep away the evil with some gesture toward the compensating goodness of God. Sin, she says, is real: it may be the source of, or even may consist in, every sort of illusion to which humans are prone, whether about themselves, about others, or about God. But there is no sort of unreality in the fact of our thus misrelating: the complex reality is that, on account of the world's sin, unreality is the pervasive medium of our actual relationships, this condition being the meaning of what Julian and Christians generally call the "Fall." And so the question that dominates her reflections is simple: Why, given a good God, who is omnipotent and all good, is there sin at all? But it is a question that calls for the resolution of a dilemma by other means than the Humean elimination of one of its horns. The propositions that the omnipotent and unfailing love of God created the world, and that there is sin, are, she believes, both undeniably true. There is, for Julian, no simplifying Humean way out of the apparent conflict between them. So then what?

Most philosophers of our times in the Christian tradition seem to think it just eccentric to raise the question "Why is there sin?" that Julian sees is forced upon her in consequence of her insisting that her dilemma cannot be resolved by simply cutting off one of its horns. And it is worth noting why her question seems so important to her and so odd to the philosophers and theologians today. For the assumption widespread among those who concern themselves with such issues, whether philosophers or theologians, is that the one thing for which you don't need an explanation is that sin happens and is bound to. It seems to them, as it did to Hume, too obvious to be worth debating that if you create a world of free agents, where freedom must at least allow for the choice between good and evil actions, then necessarily some evil choices are going to be made.[12] Nor is that "necessarily" a hyperbolic statement of what is no more than a very strong likelihood. For it is a view almost universally maintained among philosophers that although a world of completely free agents none of whom ever choose evil actions is certainly describable, by strict logical necessity such a world is uncreatable even by an almighty God. For, it is argued, were God to cause such a world to exist, then God's causing there to be no sinful choices in it would thereby rob those innocent choices of their freedom, it being assumed that no action of mine can be free if any one or thing other than myself is the cause of it. And that "anything other" includes God. A world without sin, though it may be described, is therefore impossible to create even for an omnipotent Creator. Necessarily, then, there is sin because God cannot create a world guaranteed to be without it, and Julian's question "Why is there sin?" is redundant. Such is the view of the Calvinist philosopher Alvin Plantinga.[13]

But Julian insists: God could have created not only that world of free human beings in which *as it happens* no one sins, but a world *such that* no one freely chooses to sin. In fact there is a vast spiritual, as well as intellectual, chasm between Plantinga, who evidently thinks that the human will could be free only if it occupies a space evacuated of the divine causal agency, and the medieval anchoress, for whom, as for Augustine and Aquinas, our free choices are precisely where the presence of God's agency is most evidently and directly working. You can see God acting directly in our free actions, so Augustine and Aquinas say, for precisely insofar as they are free they are not subject to determination by natural causes: between my will, its free causality, and God's agency nothing intervenes. It is true that God's acting in the natural world is always indirect, for there it is always mediated by natural, worldly causes. For it may be that nature, as Gerard Manley Hopkins put it, is charged with "God's grandeur"; but the visibility of God is there reflected, as the medieval theologians put it, as in a mirror, there seen not directly, not immediately, as it is in our free actions. By contrast it is just because of her view that God is the direct and unmediated cause of our free choices that Julian thinks that there is a real question why God did not create a world of free agents who freely choose not to sin. As Julian sees it, God could have done so. And so she tells us that "I saw that nothing stood in my way but sin. And I saw that this was so for us all generally, and I thought: if there had been no sin we should all have been clean and like to the Lord who made us. And thus . . . I often wondered why by the great foresight and wisdom of God sin had not been prevented. For then, I thought all should have been well."[14]

Christian theologians, especially those who seek that escape route between the horns of Hume's dilemma known as the "free-will defense," should give serious thought to Julian's doubt here. One of the reasons why Julian ought to be a much tougher theological read than the cheerful and empty-headed goody-two-shoes she is too often represented as being in some pious Christian circles today is that today's readers fail to advert to how far she is from pursuing the escape route out of the problem of sin available in Plantinga's conventional account. Julian would have been much puzzled by Plantinga's ploy; indeed, she would have been much troubled by a view of how the divine causality stands to free human choices according to which they are mutually exclusive. For Plantinga, if I did it freely, then necessarily God was not the cause of my doing it. For Julian, as again for Augustine and Thomas, to think like Plantinga of God's causality as excluding my free action, in the sort of way in which your jogging my elbow would thus far exclude my spilling of the tea as being a free act, is fundamentally to misrepresent the nature of the divine causality in its relation to human freedom.

Such is at root Hume's mistake too. The reason why his skeptical arguments fail as refutations of theism, that is, upon the ground of the incompatibility of moral evil with the goodness of God, is the same as the reason why Plantinga's "free-will defense" fails. In either case the same conception of God's relationship to human freedom is represented as one of mutual exclusion. To construe the divine governance as if it were some sort of supercreaturely agency interfering in the world from outside it and competing with it is to represent that agency as a semipagan deity jogging the world's elbow at arbitrary will, rather than as the total cause creating it out of nothing, and so as being more within the world's agency and its freedom than any creaturely cause can possibly be. That divine agency is therefore more within human free agency inasmuch as it is the cause and condition of that agency's freedom. That is why God's causality is, as Augustine put it, *interior intimo meo*, "more within me than [even] I am." It is in causing the freedom of my free actions that God's presence and activity are most, not least evident. In fact, at one point Julian goes so far as to say that he, God, "is the onlie doer."[15] Unlike Plantinga, therefore, Julian sees no problem of consistency in maintaining that God could have created a world of free but sinless human beings. But just because of that, she has to face a problem that can't arise for Plantinga: since God could have created a world of free moral agents without sin, should he not have done so, she asks, since such a world would have been the best possible world; and would you not suppose that a perfectly good and all-powerful God would as a matter of course make such, and only such, a world?

IS OURS THE BEST POSSIBLE WORLD?

At this point Julian is fully engaged in a sort of dialogical argument with the Lord about the matter—chapters 27 through 32 of her Long Text read like a sort of conversational disputed question in the academic mode of the medieval university—and it is a subtle one requiring the sort of careful reading that it doesn't always get in the secondary literature. It is true that the Lord rebukes Julian for her anxieties about sin, but what she thereupon corrects herself for having thought is not that she had been wrong in supposing that God could have created a world of free human agents who did not sin but that she had been wrong in assuming that all would have been well only in such a sinless world. What the Lord tells her—as it will seem very improbably—is that all is well in just this sinful world, and that puzzles her all the more. For in recounting this episode in her showings Julian admits she needed persuading of how what she is told could be true, for manifestly this world of sin could not be the best possible world, for the removal from it of just one unnecessarily cruel act would make it at least that much better. So why would God create a lesser good when a better, indeed best, world was available for the creating? Her conclusion is, sensibly enough, that no world could answer to the description "best possible," any more than a sonnet or a string quartet could answer to the description "best possible" sonnet or string quartet.

Of course there is the view that for a theist there must be a best possible string quartet, namely the string quartet that God would compose were God to compose one, for God couldn't compose a quartet that would be in any way less than the best possible. In fact, even were there such a piece of music as the best possible string quartet, God could not be under any constraint to compose only it, because if God can compose only the best possible string quartet, then there is something that Beethoven can do that God cannot. For while Beethoven could compose his C# minor string quartet Opus 131 (he did), it would follow on this account that God could not have composed it, because even were the C# minor quartet the best string quartet now going (it is), obviously the C# minor string quartet is not the best *possible* string quartet. There is at least possibly a better one on the cards, even a better one that Beethoven himself might have composed had he lived.[16]

And as it is with string quartets, so it is with worlds. Like Thomas Aquinas, Julian does not think this is the best possible world.[17] Like any medieval Christian believer, she thinks a world is possible in which, like ours, everybody is totally free and in which, unlike ours, everyone is of such a mind that sinning does not and cannot come into the picture any more, and its being so is exactly as God has omnipotently willed it, since God has created exactly that state of affairs in creating the heaven that is offered to us after death. If we make it there we are guaranteed for all eternity to be utterly sinless and utterly free in our not sinning. So it is not on account of her being at odds with Plantinga's style of defense that Julian is rebuked, because the Lord evidently agrees with Julian rather than Plantinga on the score of his having the power to create a sinless world of free agents. Rather, she is rebuked for her having supposed that "all manner of things [would be] well" only in such a sinless world. In any case it remains the case that even heaven is not the best possible state of affairs, not because heaven fails to be as good as it could be, but because there isn't any condition answering to the description "best possible world" that heaven fails to instantiate.

THE "BEHOVELY"

What Julian is told is that in this world in which there is all the sin that there is, with all its "sharp pain," nothing is "amiss" and that in just that world sin is "behovabil" (as the later Sloane text puts it using a now redundant Middle English word) or "behovely" (as the earlier Paris MS has it). And Plantinga comes into the picture here for a very particular reason having to do with the mistranslation of those words into modern English that is to be found in the older Penguin modernization of the Long Text by Clifton Wolters and, more alarmingly, even in the more scholarly Colledge and Walsh modernized version. "Sin is necessary" is how all three have it. Necessarily, then, in a world of free agents there will be sin. So Wolters. So Colledge and Walsh. That translation, however, yields Plantinga. It is not what Julian says.

Why is it so egregiously wrong to translate *behovely* as "necessary" in the way Wolters and Colledge and Walsh do on lexical grounds, and as Plantinga would require as a matter of logic? The reason is that this translation of *behovely* involves a misunderstanding of the nature of the theological predicament that Julian feels constrained to address. For, as we have seen, "necessary" is exactly what Julian thinks sin is not: that is why, believing that things could have been otherwise, she has the problem Plantinga does not have, and why she cannot go along with his kind of solution, or anything like it. She needs to take an entirely different theological tack.

"Necessary" won't do as a translation of *behovely* because *necessary* is a term forming a joint in a linear, inferential, that is, logical sequence: if this is the case, then necessarily that follows. And the way of understanding sin as being "necessary" would appear to be attractive to those for whom, maintaining that there could not be a creatable world without sin, a philosophical solution to the problem of evil is thereby made available: since evil is necessary in any world that God can actually create, God can't help it if there is sin. But Julian thinks there is no solution by such means, and her approach to the problem evokes a quite different vocabulary of explanation. Just as the logician's "Necessarily if p then q" has a formal constructive character within the inferentially linear, so Julian's "It is behovely that there is sin" has a formal, constructive character in relation to the quite distinct literary structure of the narrative. In short, *behovely* is connective tissue of a story line, not of a syllogism.

As a rough translation into modern English, Julian's *behovely* means something like "fitting," or "befitting," implying that there is something that the behovely fits with and gets its sense from; or perhaps "appropriate," which, likewise, needs a context within which it has a well-judged narrative presence; or, as I would have it, "just so." And to get closest to a distinctly medieval meaning of *behovely*, the best translation is not into modern English at all, but rather into a medieval Latin term of theological art, namely, *conveniens*. One way of getting a grip on the praeter-logical

character of the term is from a standard medieval question about the Incarnation: "Whether the Incarnation was necessary?"—to which the standard answer from the time of Anselm's late eleventh-century treatise
known as *Why Did God Become Man?* was twofold. No, the Incarnation,
absolutely speaking was not necessary: God, after all, was not under any
necessity of nature or any obligation in justice to do anything at all about
the sinful predicament of creatures; and, if he were to do anything about
it, many possibilities of relieving that predicament were available to God
besides the Incarnation—and, what is more still, all of them at lower cost.
Yet the second person of the Trinity, the Word, was made flesh and dwelt
among us. Why?

Duns Scotus was to say early in the fourteenth century that God became man not as a response required by an event unanticipated, not, or at
any rate not principally, as a solution to any kind of problem, because
Scotus thought that even had Adam not sinned, God just fancied the idea
of becoming man regardless; as Proverbs puts it, it was Wisdom's "delight
to be with the children of men."[18] On the other hand, if God was under
no constraint of necessity to become man, neither was the Incarnation
a merely contingent whim on the part of God to send his Son into the
world, to preach and suffer and die for the world's sake. If neither under
any necessity to do so nor, in doing so, merely whimsically indulging his
power to do it, then the question why God chose to set in train just those
events, historically particular as they were and are, needs to be understood
otherwise than in terms of logical or natural necessity. We need instead a
vocabulary of answers to the question "Why did such and such happen?"
that is closer to a vocabulary in which one answers for an event's occurrence within a particular narrative of events—because one is explaining
how the narrative makes sense of just that and only that happening. And,
as to the Incarnation, the term of art that, after Anselm, the medieval theologians used in answering the question why God became man was that it
was *conveniens*. What was done was done, the medieval theologians said,
not as if by accident or on a whim or just by happenstance. Nor was it a
sort of Plan B, things having gone so terribly wrong with Plan A in the
Garden of Eden. But if it was on no account a necessity imposed upon
God, it was indeed "just right" that God should do it; though done in
utter freedom it was also *conveniens*, behovely, or perhaps just the thing,

a Godlike thing to do. And you can get to see how right it was if you can get the hang of the story it fits within. In short, *conveniens* in Latin, and *behovely* in Middle English, are terms descriptive not of how logical and linear, but rather of how narrative and spiral, sequences are formed. They are terms descriptive of what is just right about a good story, such that if you are to understand why this or that happened you need some access to the story that makes sense of it.

The vocabulary of the *conveniens* or the *behovely* is connective, not in the sense of extrusion along a line by means of inferential sequences, but in the sense of a narrative spiraling that accumulates meanings as it goes along and, as it accumulates those meanings, progressively demands the readjustment of the narrative curve. And that brings in all sorts of matters needing explanation, of which the first is this: whereas logic, dealing in inferential sequences, must abstract the general from the particular, narratives are always particular, individuated. You can tell that logic doesn't need the particular because it is, or can be, formalized algebraically—you don't need particular values for the variables to get the formulas of logic going, they hold for each and every substitution for p and q. But "behovely" doesn't work that way. If, as Julian believes, sin can be seen to be behovely, then this can only be because there is some narrative of everything whatever, because the sum total of things adds up to a story, to just this story of just this sequence of events, including those sins, whose place within the narrative is "fitting," "just so." For there is just one narrative of everything whatever, there is just one sum total of events that is human history, and what has happened has happened this way and not that, though it might have happened otherwise. And what is going to happen is going to happen this way rather than that, though it might have been going to happen otherwise. And what is behovely is what fits within just that particular narrative of just this world, which is the way it is because it has been created to be like that by a perfect love. And for Julian, just as for Scotus, Thomas Aquinas, and perhaps especially Dante, the trajectory through time of just this world is in this way the plot of a *commedia*. Now this seems to mean for Julian that the way to think about the world we inhabit, and the history we have made, is, in respect of this comedic character of a singularity, very much like the way one thinks about a work of art, or about a story. It is unique in the way that stories are, or a melody is, and

Julian's notion of what "fits," of what is behovely, is, in consequence, more of an aesthetic kind than a logical one.

It is perhaps easiest to see this in music, for its arrow of time is, like that of a narrative, unidirectional. A friend to whom I had been waxing on about Mozart complained that his music is "just too predictable." This seems to me to be interestingly wrong. For apart from a few standardized cadences that are a sort of musical throat-clearing, everything in Mozart's music is supremely unpredictable; but also, everything in Mozart's music is supremely retrodictable, so transparently retrodictable as to create the illusion post factum of utter predictability and obviousness. When a cadence or a modulation is completed in an unexpected way, you are surprised and yet know immediately why it had to be just so, and how its being just so reveals anew everything that precedes it. Stories and music—perhaps especially music of the classical period—in the end make the surprising turn of events to be obvious,[19] as if after the event we can see how we might have predicted it, even though before the event in no wise could we have done so.

SIN IS BEHOVELY

Some such notion of the "behovely" would assist an understanding of Julian's theology were we considering but her description of the Incarnation itself in those terms. For the coming of Christ could not have been anticipated had it not been prophesied. We had need to be told that such was on the cards, because no necessity entailed it, whether on the side of the divine or that of human justice. But when the Incarnation happens, everything comes clear. We have a new hermeneutic of the Old Law, and obscure poetry that seemed to mean one thing becomes a hermeneutical key for everything. One has only to think of how differently the prophecies of Isaiah or Ezekiel read when, post factum, they are read in light of the Incarnation: Jewish interpreters can see this very clearly, which is why they reject the reading.[20] And everything would be uncontroversial and clear as to the role of the term in Julian's theology had she merely been proposing the medieval commonplace that the Incarnation was in this way "behovely."

But the problem is that it is not all she says. What Julian says is behovely is sin. Now what are we to say about this cheerfully upbeat goody-two-shoes? The problem of credibility that Julian's theology presents us with deserves to be faced squarely. Here we have a great theologian of the Christian Church telling us that sin is behovely. She tells us this not because she is cheerfully naive about the world's evil but because, knowing the world's evil for what it is, she believes that it follows from core Christian beliefs about divine love and power that sin so "fits" with the divine plan that nothing can be "amiss."[21] And, whatever else, this is implausible, even scandalously so. For we must suppose Julian's theology to entail that behovely, and so not "amiss," was the bureaucratic cold efficiency with which the murder of six million Jews was planned and executed; behovely, the ideologically motivated mass exterminations of the Pol Pot regime; behovely, the frenzied pogroms of Rwanda and the mass rapes of Syria; behovely, the betrayals of every adulterous spouse; behovely, every politician's lie told in breach of voters' trust; behovely, every sexual abuse of a child; behovely, every rich person's denial of food to the hungry. If these are not amiss, would it not seem that nothing could be amiss and that Julian's response to the problem of evil is simply to deny, a priori and in the face of the overwhelming weight of evidence to the contrary, that there is any possible evil that could be a problem for belief in God?

It has to be admitted that at this sort of point in the argument it is all too easy for contemporary theologians to lose their nerve—and it would seem to be on account of such moral panic that the free-will defense of Plantinga and others can seem to be the only way out for believers; you take Plantinga's line in order not to be stuck with Julian's and because you feel weighed down by the heavy burden of human evil. If all you need say is that evils of such incalculable extent and intensity can't be helped, they wouldn't be sins if they were not freely done, and our not sinning would not be free if God had prevented it, then you cannot blame God for sin, it's all our fault and none of it is down to God. So it is said as if to make it theologically all right, since the only way in which there could be a world without sin would be in a world that was without humans, occupied only by automata preprogrammed by God. A sinless world is impossible given human freedom, and without freedom there are no human beings.

For Julian such a conception of God and human freedom is not all right. Significantly, Julian's position is closer to that of most atheists of our times than it is to that of most contemporary Christian theologians.

Here is Plantinga again: "It was beyond the power of God himself to create a world containing moral good but no moral evil."[22] Julian disagrees: God could have created such a world and did not. Then there is John Mackie, an atheist precisely on account of believing Julian to be right and Plantinga wrong: "God was not . . . faced with the choice between making innocent automata and making beings who, in acting freely, would sometimes go wrong: there was open to him the obviously better possibility of making beings who would act freely but always go right. Clearly [God's] failure to avail himself of this possibility is inconsistent with his being both omnipotent and wholly good."[23] And here again is the stubborn Julian, the fourteenth-century anchoress, sorely tempted to agree with Mackie: "And I thought that if sin had never existed, we should all have been pure and like himself, as God made us; and so in my folly I had often wondered before now, why, in his great foreseeing wisdom, God had not prevented the beginning of sin; for then, I thought, all would have been well."[24] What is clear, then, is that, to put it all in anachronistic terms, Julian would rather have Mackie's problem, with or without a solution, than be forced to conclude in the terms that Plantinga does, the price of which solution would have to be paid in the currency of what a later age called "deism," the doctrine of a God whose presence is expelled from that part of the creation that for her is most in his image and likeness, the human freedom of choice. That conclusion Julian cannot tolerate, and it is not hard to see why. For in truth there is no solution in Plantinga's deism that differs in any significant way from Hume's theological skepticism. Both have to take God out of the picture, at any rate of human freedom.

So does Julian have a solution? She makes it quite clear that neither she nor anyone else is in possession of one. But certainly she knows there is a solution, for "all manner of thing will be well," and, what is more, she knows what alone could count as a solution. Much depends on how we are to understand her when at the very end of her second attempt at the problem, in the work that we know of as her Long Text, after perhaps more than twenty years of turning the problem of sin over and around, she tells us in the last chapter of the Long Text that though "this book was begun by God's gift and his grace . . . [it] is not yet performed as to my sighte."[25]

Clearly, among the things Julian does not mean by her book's being "not yet performed" is that her text, her book, is unfinished: on the contrary, the statement that her work is incomplete is clearly intended as the appropriate and responsible conclusion to as carefully constructed and complete a theological treatise as any in the fourteenth century. Nor does she mean that, though some theological progress has been made in the Long Text which she was not able to make in her earlier, much shorter version, perhaps a third attempt at it might yield a text that is finally "performed," a text that once and for all answers the question "How could a good God allow sin?" in the sense that John Milton seemed to think was required of a theologically satisfactory response; for he thought he could construct a narrative of paradise lost and regained that would be able to "justifie the wayes of God to men."[26] But if Julian does not mean that the Long Text is "not yet performed" as to its nature as a text, for as such it is undoubtedly finished, she certainly does mean that it is not "complete" in the sense that Milton thought his was, in which the occurrence and pervasiveness of sin are said to have been theologically "justified." For on her account of it no such justification of God's ways is available in principle. Therefore, in not providing one, Julian's text does not, in her view, fail of a completeness that is in any case and in principle theologically impossible. It is complete as a text because in it she demonstrates that it is necessarily incomplete theologically.

It is the "not yet" that matters here. The "book" in question is not after all hers, for it contains revelations *given* to her. The book that is not yet performed is the book of time, the book of history, and her book belongs there, incomplete as history is incomplete. It is history that is provisional, and it is in that theological refusal of both forms of theological completeness, on the one hand the "linear" completeness of the philosophical Plantinga, which would purport to demonstrate the formal consistency of an infinite love's creating just this sinful world, and, on the other hand and no less unacceptable, the completeness claimed by the poetical Milton, which would purport to "out-narrate" the problem of sin by completing the story that "justifies the wayes of God to men." For all her questions about how it could be true, Julian accepts that "sin is behovely." It's got to be. But Julian knows enough about how the logic of the behovely works—as narratives do—to know that we could see how sin could be behovely only were we in possession of the complete narrative that makes sense of it, and that we are not. What we possess is but a narrative fragment, a torn-off corner of the manuscript of salvation history, and it tells Julian of nothing but the paradox of an innocent man judicially executed for a reason he too begs to know of, though he dies, as we will, the reason why denied us all. By faith Julian knows that—though what she knows is that she does not know how—the meaning of sin, its character of the behovely, lies in that incomplete narrative of the cross that is at the heart of her showings, a narrative whose incompleteness is necessary, for "not yet" belongs to the nature of human existence in time.

Julian, then, cannot complete the "book," for incompleteness is in the nature of the narrative spiral itself. It is not just sin's being behovely that is being told by that narrative, it is she—we—who are being told by it, including her two attempts to grapple with that narrative fragment that is shown to her. In that fragment is the meaning, but it is hidden from her; it is, she says, "a great secret."[27] Julian knows that her attempts to lay hold of the complete story are themselves but episodes within it, or, as the postmodernists of our times would have it, she is being read by the narratives she believes herself to be writing, she is being told by the narrative she twice attempts to tell. What would answer Julian's question "Why sin?" is the narrative completed, her book performed. And that cannot be done within history, in time. For the completed narrative is, literally, "end of story," and that, Julian knows, is the beatific vision, the price of which is death.

In the meantime, then, there is but the meantime, the "not yet." And Julian does her theology, she twice writes her *Revelation of Love*, and she lives the life of the anchoress, all of these obedient to that condition of incompleteness, obedient to a condition in which neither understanding nor living can yet be "performed." Julian is the theologian she is because she knows that theology is writing as penultimate, and she refuses Hume's easygoing and yet peremptory closure. For writing that is pretentiously "finished" is not theological, it is parody, it is Jeremy Bentham's "nonsense upon stilts," the ridiculous parading as the sublime. Julian's theology is truly spiral. It begins and ends where unending begins. And maybe T. S. Eliot in *Four Quartets* did get it right, at any rate he got it from his reading of Julian. For her as for Eliot, in her end is her beginning. If we knew where Harvard was, we would know how to journey there, even if perforce the journey had to begin from Princeton.

TWO

"One with God as to the Unknown"

Prayer and the Darkness of God

I invite you today to give thought to a rather surprising statement that Thomas Aquinas makes toward the beginning of his *Summa theologiae*. For some it might even be disturbing, and I too was a little taken aback when I first discovered him saying that "[even] by the revelation of grace we do not know what God is; and so it is that [by grace] we are joined to [God] as to one unknown [to us]."[1] He does not say, "God is hard to know, you have to work at it," or "God is elusive" or "evasive," but simply: what God is, what kind of thing God is, is unknown to us, even by faith.

It is true that the full text of the passage provides context and an important qualification, a qualification that I shall come to in due course. But as it stands—and despite that qualification Thomas does let it stand— by any measure it is a startlingly agnostic statement. I imagine it would be less shocking to modern theological minds had Thomas said only that God's nature is unknown to us by way of our theologically limited powers of natural reason. That, after all, is a proposition that a modern theologian in the spirit of Karl Barth would have been only too pleased to endorse, had Thomas allowed that if not by reason then by faith God's nature is made known to us. But that is not what Thomas says. He says that God's nature is unknown to us *even* within the revelation of grace.

WE DO NOT KNOW WHAT GOD IS

Ever the deadpan writer and teacher even (or perhaps especially) when at his most theologically radical, Thomas tells us this in an article of the *Summa* in which he asks whether grace affords us a higher knowledge of God than that which can be had by our natural, unaided powers of reason. In the dialectical manner that he employs for such discussions, Thomas first addresses the view to which in due course he will say he is opposed. He asks: Is there not a case to be made for the view that the revelation of grace gets us no further into the knowledge of God than does the reach of reason alone?

You might reasonably have thought you could guess where Thomas would go with this: he will say, you imagined, that of course the grace of faith draws us further into the knowledge of God than reason by its own powers can. But he doesn't say this, not yet, he wants to hold back a minute, for there are powerful objections to any such proposition, one of them supplied by the fifth-century Syrian monk known today as the pseudo-Denys, who tells us that though what in this life unites us best to God is grace, still even by grace we are made one with God as to a being whose nature, he says, is *omnino ignota*, "altogether unknown" to us. Hence, the grace of revelation gains no better traction on God than what bare reason anyway affords us: in either case we are left in the dark as to what God is, we are wandering as it were without intellectual bearings, lost in a cloud of unknowing.

But that is not all, Thomas adds, for it is on scripture, on the witness of Moses no less, that the pseudo-Denys relies when he so emphatically teaches of this God beyond all knowing—Thomas doesn't say exactly where scripture records this, but doubtless he is thinking here, as elsewhere he says he is, of the great epiphany recorded in Exodus 33:17–23. There we are told that, having ascended to the summit of Mount Sinai shrouded in a cloud of unknowing, Moses is instructed by Yahweh to hide himself in the cleft of a rock so as not to see the Lord's face when he passes by. For seeing the face of God is dangerous, you need to be dead and under special conditions of God-given vision thereafter, which is why while you are alive the face of God would kill you were you to be exposed to it. For "no one may see my face and live."

This is strong stuff open to no qualification, and most theologians seem not to take it all that seriously, supposing that "negative theology" is some sort of spiritual fashion statement, splendidly dramatic but optional, a preference for those of an austere taste in matters epistemological. Many do seem to think that once you get the hang of theological talk, then, if not by way of reason, maybe from the Bible, and certainly in Christ, God is as routinely knowable in, say, the practices of Christian worship as "the man in the street along." But Thomas will not have it so. The weight of biblical authority exerts heavy pressure on claims to such cheap and easily acquired knowledge of God: before the transcendence of God faith is every bit as benighted as is reason, and Thomas is going to have to make concessions to that biblical authority. And so he does. Let us first yield to the authority of Exodus, he says, and then to that of the pseudo-Denys, who, along with most of his fellow theologians of his time Thomas regarded as possessing an authority only a little less than the Bible's; and let us accept what it tells us, howsoever severely economical it may epistemologically seem — for that statement, he says, stands, come what may. Having said which he then puzzlingly would seem to say the contrary, adding that by grace "we do know [God] more fully insofar as [by grace] we are shown more of his effects and higher ones; and that is so inasmuch as on the basis of revelation we make some attributions of [God] of a kind unavailable to reason, such as that God is three and one."

The whole passage — it's all in a tiny response to an objection — now stands before us, and it is hard to make out where the consistency lies. The bold and unqualified agnostic statement emphatically reaffirmed as it stands is supplemented by a qualification tacked on to it that seems to contradict it. In particular it is puzzling in that it might seem to amount both to affirming something, namely that we do not know what God is, and then, scarcely a breath taken, to denying it with an implied "nonetheless." "Nonetheless," Thomas says, God is known *better* by faith than by reason. Well then, one or the other, either we do know God, what he is, or we don't. If we know God better by faith and somehow less well by reason, then implied is the proposition that even by reason we do know at least something about what God is, even if not very much. And that doesn't seem to fit with the bald statement with which the passage begins: whether by reason or by faith we do not know what God is, God's nature is to us *omnino ignota*. The argument is evidently in need of some clarification. So let us try to clarify.

Let us allow the agnostic statement to stand: we do not know what God is. Whatever else he is going on to say, Thomas holds on to that proposition, and you can get his drift along some such lines as these. We human beings are worldly creatures, we are, after all, animals, environmentally locked into a material ecosystem with which, by way of our essential embodiment, we are finely calibrated: we need an environmental temperature sustained within strict limits, and we are, as we all now know, worryingly close to them. In that universe of experience, in the material world to which our lives, and our minds, are thus naturally attuned, we can get to know any individual thing with which our senses acquaint us in its distinct individuality—*this* tree, *this* person, *my* wife, or *each* one of you—only under some description of the kind of thing that each one of us is an individual instance of. I cannot know just "this individual, whatever-it-is doesn't matter."[2] I can know only this individual who is this person, or this woman, or this lump of wood that is this tree. That is, individuals fall under descriptions, they come in kinds, the "this" depends on the "what," for I can experience this individual only insofar as I find a particular place for it within a worldly context of meaning, within an ecology, or, as we say, an environment.

Such thoughts are worth giving time and space to in an individualist culture such as ours, for which what is primary, and from an explanatory point of view the more fundamental—or even on some accounts, also from an existential point of view more basic—is a pure abstraction known as "the individual." As Herbert McCabe used to say, maybe for a modern mind in the West it seems intuitive that societies are made of individuals; but it isn't intuitive at all, it's the construction of a theory that has become the truism of a culture, a bit of ideology that, until the emergence of a nominalist and in consequence an individualist culture in the late medieval and early modern periods, no patristic or early medieval theologian would have found convincing. At any rate for Thomas the prior truth is the opposite, namely that individuals are made of the social relations in which they are born, grow, learn to speak, have sex, give birth, love, and die, and therein is the paradox of modernity: it takes a certain form of society to make its individualism seem intuitively obvious; and once you see that "the individual" is a social construct you can see that there is no prior individualist intuition there anyway, but only a socially acquired moral and ideological preference. An ontological individualism according to which the basic and irreducible existent is "the individual" is as much a social construction as any other, and a more counterintuitively constructed abstraction than many.

This thought may itself seem a bit abstract, but in truth it is simple. I love my wife. I love her in her individuality of course, but just as obviously I love her in her individual womanhood, so that how I love her individually will depend in part upon how far I successfully grasp her construction of that womanhood. Of course I love her for who she is, but it won't be her I love if I do not love her for what she is—that knowledge and love of who inextricably tied in with the what, the two together. That's just how we love.

When therefore Jews, Christians, and Muslims say, as they all do, that there is "but one God," the ultimate and complete object of our knowledge and love, they immediately cause themselves a problem precisely arising from this insistence that they do not know what God is. They say that they are commanded to love God, or as Thomas says, to be united with him, not knowing what they love. So how can they know how to love? For if there is no knowable kind of thing that God is, then it would seem to follow that in the case of God you cannot get the distinction to work between what God is and who God is so as to love the "who." For there is no kind of thing, Thomas says, of which the one God is the only instance. And if that is so we are compelled to wonder what meaning can be rescued of the word *one* as designating "this" God, the God of any of the Abrahamic faiths, Jewish, Christian, or Muslim.

To be sure, Thomas cannot find himself going down the line of supposing that Jewish or Muslim insistence on the oneness of God is somehow less mysterious than the Christian insistence on the Trinitarian threeness. The truth is, Thomas says, that whether by God's oneness or by God's threeness we are equally benighted, dumfounded, drawn into that cloud of unknowing that sits forever on the summit of Mount Sinai where God dwells. For if we can say for certain that there is only one God, it is also true that we have lost track of the meaning of the word *one* in so saying. In that case, how should we love God? asks another Dominican—indeed, how could we love so unknowable a God? And that other Dominican replies: "You should love God unspiritually. . . . You should love him as a non-God, a nonspirit, a nonperson, a nonimage, but as he is a pure un-mixed bright One, separated from all duality; and in that One we should eternally sink down, out of 'something' into 'nothing.' May God help us to that. Amen."[3]

That Dominican of course is not Thomas. It is Meister Eckhart writing some forty years or so after Thomas's death. It is not how Thomas himself ultimately concludes, as we will see. But it is a pretty accurate statement of where Thomas is at the end of question 2 of the first part of the *Summa*. For there he says that you should not suppose even the arguments that show God to exist to have got us anywhere near knowing *what* God is: the hopes for such knowledge are vain and must be quickly and firmly disap-pointed. And in a truly magnificent act of theological self-denial, one that should put to shame the uncritical theological optimists of our times, Thomas affirms in his deadpan academic manner exactly what Eckhart says in his rolling homiletic rhetoric: "Since it is not possible to know of God what he is, we cannot give thought to the manner of God's existence, but only to how God is not."[4]

HOW THEN WE DO KNOW THAT GOD IS?

As I say, all this can come as a bit of a surprise for believers, even as a shock, for it would seem to push God away as a being wholly remote, in-accessible to all human experience, hardly the God they say they come to know in the intimacy of the person of Christ. And anyway many will won-der, very reasonably, how Thomas can say that we do not know what God is consistently with also saying, as he does at the very beginning of the *Summa*, that we can by means of five strategies of demonstration prove God's existence.[5] And, what would seem more problematic still, Thomas says that we can prove God's existence without any appeal to faith or reve-lation or to anything other than plain secular reason. But how can this be?

The case for saying that God's existence can be proved—"Deum esse probari potest," he says—would seem to sit ill with not knowing what God is. Eat your cake—God's nature is unknowable—if you must; but if so, how can you also have it if, consistently with God's nature being beyond our ken, you can nonetheless rationally prove God's existence?

The dilemma, thus somewhat oversimplified, causes some today to hold fast to one horn of it at the expense of the other. In fact for some decades there seems to have been agreement among a majority of readers of the *Summa* that Thomas could not have really meant it when he said that his five ways are knockdown arguments, valid and sound, proving God's existence on purely rational grounds. He simply must have meant something logically weaker than "rationally proved," for a proof of God's existence that was purely rational would reduce God to the standing of just another item in the universe, making a God out of a creature, or a creature out of God. That would certainly be idolatrous, and such an argument would do the opposite of rationally proving the existence of God. It would, rather more simply, make a God out of rational proof. And at once, having seen that, you begin to see how close the early nineteenth-century atheist Ludwig Feuerbach cut to the Christian bone when he said that all the atheist has to do to defeat the Christian argument for God is to turn it upside down. Such arguments prove human reason to be subjectively godlike and infinite; they do not, as such theists suppose, prove that reason shows there to be an infinite being objectively divine. The logic here is common ground between the Feuerbachian atheist and the antirationalist theist: the God that reason can prove to exist is contained within the limits of the reason that constructs the proof. A God of the proofs is simply not God at all.

I am unconvinced. You can easily turn this argument on its head: only suppose you could prove the existence of God, an unknowable God whose nature is altogether beyond our power of understanding, *omnino ignota,* as the pseudo-Denys said; would that not show something about reason, namely that a rational proof is not after all a limitation imposed on God? Rather would it not show the opposite, that is, that reason, pushed all the way along its trajectory of questioning and explaining the world, breaks out on the other side of its limits into the boundless mystery of an unknowable God? The notion that reason, at any rate in its speculative and inferential mode, can operate only within a finite circle, forming an arc that endlessly returns upon itself, thus to enclose in its finitude all that falls within its remit, seems wrongly to explain what Thomas means by the word. It is certainly an idea of reason that is recognizable in much Enlightenment thinking. It is there in Kant. But it is nowhere to be found in Thomas.

For, as Thomas understands it, reason's trajectory is neither circular nor in any other way closed: or, if it has the character of the circular in any way at all, it is as spirals are circular, a circularity that is also extruded out into an open and unending linearity. For, as the pseudo-Denys says, theology proceeds neither in a circle nor in a straight line only, but most distinctively in that combination of both at once, which is the spiral with neither beginning nor end. Therefore, just as Thomas asserts the demonstrability of God's existence so also does he make himself quite clear: by way of those proofs our minds are opened up to something altogether beyond our comprehension, and it is that incomprehensible "something" which, Thomas says with characteristic brevity, "all people call by the name of God." It is far from it being the case, then, as some have seemed to suppose, that the five ways draw God back into the closed circle of reason. They do exactly the opposite: they show, Thomas thinks, that reason itself, by way of its own characteristic exercise of proof, breaks through its own comfort zone and enters into the mystery of the Godhead, which lies entirely beyond its own limits. Thus do the apophatic biblical instincts of Exodus and Isaiah converge with the result of rational argument upon the one mystery of God.

Reason, then, Thomas says, is, in its culminating theological act, self-dissolving; it meets its own apotheosis by, as Hegel put it, abolishing itself in its very act of self-realization. And in that self-dissolution it leads us into that dark mystery that is God. It is just on that account that Thomas shuts the door so firmly on any kind of know-all theology, or, as we should say in a more biblical manner of speech, any form of idolatry. In particular it shuts the door on a God, as Immanuel Kant was centuries later to put it, "within the bounds of reason." For Thomas, the proofs of the existence of God show that at the end of the line, there escaping the grip of reason, is ungraspable mystery: what most exists, that which sustains all other realities in existence, is unknowable. And then one needs to add, as Thomas will go on to show, that the mystery has a name: the true name of that mystery is "love."

FAITH AND THE DARKNESS OF GOD

What, then, of faith? Here too Thomas might seem to be caught in a dilemma parallel to that in which it seemed reason was entangled, as if again he was attempting to have it both ways at once. For having said not only that reason must fail of the knowledge of God's nature but that faith does so too, nonetheless he goes on to say that somehow faith supplies some knowledge of God that to reason is denied. And in a certain sense that is true, but not the obvious sense. For it transpires that what Thomas means is that faith does not dispel the darkness of God, for on the contrary, in faith one enters more deeply into that darkness, not escaping it, not dispelling it, but intensifying it. It is not after all very difficult to see what he is getting at in so saying, for if it is a paradox it is a paradox with a parallel in common, secular experience. Of course every human person is a mystery in herself, and no matter whom I observe in the bus or at the railway station or in the street I know that much about them, for their being a mystery simply goes with the fact of their being persons. I know *that* each person is a mystery to someone. But as to your life partner, the years of your intimacy with her will but draw you ever deeper into that heady unknowing which is love, a love that is not therefore a failure of knowledge but rather a knowledge which, born of a love in a common life shared, also allows her always to exist beyond her lover's grasp, not possessed but free and unconstrained, as only lovers are to one another, in an intimacy and objectivity perfectly aligned. That, Thomas says, is the way in which through faith we know more of God than reason knows.

And that is why, Thomas says, it is through faith that we know the Trinity, of which by reason we can never know, even if by reason we can know that God is one. Is the doctrine of the Trinity, known by faith, grounded in more information about God, information of the sort you might have gained about people passing by in the street when you have checked out the statistics: that woman is black, so her income is predictably 20 percent or more below that of the white man next to her in the same job, and she is likely to feel oppressed by an unjust disparity? Not so: the doctrine of the Trinity is not a bit of additional information about God, additional, that is, to what we can know of God by reason. Faith doesn't add something else to our rationally acquired knowledge of God.

It deepens it. It doesn't help one understand this relation between reason and faith to make out the distinction, as did some theologians in the late Middle Ages—and most do to this day—to be that between a detached, objective, dispassionate, and uninvolved reason, contrasted with what was called an *intellectus amoris*, "love's understanding" acquired in faith. William of St. Thierry had said in the twelfth century that "amor ipse intellectus est," love is its own manner of knowing, of which intellect knows nothing, and today there are many who likewise are tempted to follow down that sort of line as a way of distinguishing between reason and faith.

In fact one of Thomas's own students, Giles of Rome, yields to the temptation, saying that there is the contemplation of God, typical of the philosophers, which is of detached intellect, uninvolved and objective, and that it contrasts with the higher knowledge of the theologians, which "is more a matter of experience than of wisdom's expertise; and it consists more in loving and in sweetness than in philosophical contemplation."[6] But in advance Thomas the teacher had already firmly slapped the temptation down to which his student Giles yields, not because he thinks that *all* knowledge worth having is dispassionate and objectively cold and detached, exercised as we say in a "brown study," but for the opposite reason, namely that for him *none* is. Thomas thinks of intellect, even of reason unaided by faith, as a hot passion that seeks out the truth with intensity. He is after all a Dominican whose motto is *Veritas*, Truth, which Dominicans connected in their persons with "the way" and "the life," as did the Lord they followed. Besides, Thomas's Latin word *studium* means nothing like our modern English word *study*. Thomas's *studium* means the intense and insatiable desire for knowledge and wisdom, it denotes a passion; our word *study* is closer to denoting the uninspired dispassion, at its worst, of the pedant.

That said, anyone who has tried reading the first part of the *Summa theologiae*, questions 27 through 43 on the theology of the Trinity, might seem to be justifiably skeptical: those questions are replete with technical distinctions between persons, properties, relations, appropriations, and processions, and with complex mappings of all these upon one another in ways that in their conceptual complexity set them well outside the intellectual range of any but a hard-nosed specialist with a very high IQ. Brown indeed is the hue of those Trinitarian discussions in the *Summa*.

And yet the doctrine of the Trinity is at the center of the Christian faith and practice. How so?

The French Catholic existentialist Gabriel Marcel once said that one should never confuse a mystery with a problem. A problem asks for a solution, a solution that resolves the problem; and if you are bright enough, or conduct enough research, or consult those who know, you will find the solution to it, like the solution to a quadratic equation: once solved, the problem is laid to rest. But mysteries do not yield to investigation, argument, proof, or categorization. Mysteries can never be solved. They cannot be gotten to go away. Indeed, the deeper you enter into a mystery, the deeper the mystery gets. The gap between where you are with it and where the mystery lies never decreases, it only ever increases; nor can you think your way out of a mystery, for to do so is to reduce the mystery to the standing of a problem. But if you cannot think your way out of a mystery you can pray your way into one. Indeed, prayer is the only way there is into a mystery. Before a true mystery, the mind can only give way. You can't crack it, you can only surrender to it, and the mind boggles—you bow before it and you say, humbly, "Amen." For, strangely, in finding your way into a mystery you come to know it in a manner that no solution to a problem ever achieves. You know a mystery and you love it as you know and love a friend, you want to live with it: you can even, if you are a medieval monk or nun reading the Song of Songs, want to be kissed by it and make love together with it.[7] Problems, by contrast, are a curse until they are dissolved.

So it is with the mystery of the Trinity. And that is why, if upon reading that first part of the *Summa* on the Trinity you might understandably feel constrained to complain that it makes the fatal mistake of reducing the mystery of the Trinity to an agenda of problems you can crack, it would be a mistake to think that way. For you would be right to suppose that Thomas there constructs a technical apparatus governing how to think about the mystery of the Trinity insofar as you can—or, perhaps better, that what he offers is a structure of reflection that will enable you to avoid making obvious theological mistakes of a kind that could lead you in no time at all into dogmatic error.

Generally speaking, I am sure that G. K. Chesterton is right. It is not the likes of Thomas but the heretics who want to reduce the mysteries to problems, as, for example, Arianism does. It is after all so much easier to suppose that Christ was nothing but a man anyway, and so that he "once was not" (as the Arians would have it), than to suppose that the eternal Word of God became a man: Arius in fact didn't even want a problem to stand in his way of understanding Christ, never mind a mystery. And you could say that all that dry-as-dust apparatus of distinction and relation in Thomas's Trinitarian theology is in no way meant to crack open the mystery of the Godhead, three in one. His theology of the Trinity in the first part of the *Summa* undertakes a simple and unambitious, if very important, task, that, namely, of clearing the space of mere problems that would obstruct our access to the deep mystery of God's inner life as revealed to us in Christ. That technical metatheology does not do the substantive theology of the Trinity. It creates the space for it, space that, as Thomas shows in the *Summa*'s third part, is best filled by prayer. That discussion of the Trinity in Part I of the *Summa* is a kind of textbook of theological grammar: prayer, on the other hand, is a grammatically correct sentence uttered in conversation within the faith and love of the Trinity.

And that is why it is so obviously true that no one could preach a sermon sourced out of Thomas's Trinitarian theology in the *Summa*'s first part, and why it is true that as it stands it tells us nothing about prayer. But the impression that the *Summa* nowhere provides either source material for preaching on the Trinity or any theology of prayer is mistaken. As to the preaching, if any theologian knows about that subject, Thomas does. He is a Dominican after all, and, as Herbert McCabe used to say about his ministry, Dominicans don't pray, they preach—which doesn't mean, obviously, that Dominicans don't pray. Of course they do, any Christian does. But not all Christians go in for preaching as a way of holiness, which is what Dominicans especially do. And as to prayer as a common practice of all those who preach, it is often forgotten and rarely remarked that uniquely among medieval compilers of theological summaries Thomas offers not just that formal treatise on the Trinity in the first part of the *Summa*, or only a formal treatise on the Incarnation in its third part: for capping those schematic and formal outlines of the mysteries of God in God's own self and in Christ, Thomas offers in the third part of the *Summa* an unprecedented discussion of the central episodes, or "mysteries" as he calls them, of the historical life of Jesus. These are consciously designed preaching materials for novices in the Order of Preachers. Step by step,

Thomas recounts in over five hundred columns of narrative theology the story of Jesus's life—his conception in the womb of Mary, his birth, his baptism, his temptations, his exchanges with fellow human beings, his preaching, his miracles, his passion, his death, his burial, his descent into hell, his resurrection, his ascension, and his exaltation on the right hand of his Father. This is a fusion, found in no other theologian before him and in few since, of the theologically systematic and the narratively homiletic;[8] it is a Life of Christ in which Thomas says he will give an "account of the things that the Son of God did or suffered in his human nature." And so he does. Central to Thomas's story of the human life of Christ are two discussions of how the historical Jesus prayed. It is there, in those discussions of the man Jesus's prayer, that Thomas brings his teaching on the Trinity into the center of the Christian life.

PRAYER

When Thomas writes about prayer in general, as he does in the second part of the *Summa*, he means something more specific than we commonly refer to by our very generic English word for it, which today includes all sorts of different speech acts: thanking God, praising God, meditating about God, contemplating God, asking God, expressing before God our contrition, sadness, joy, anger even. In fact the panoply of human conversational styles falls under the word *prayer* as we today construe it, just so long as they are all forms of address to God.

By contrast with our modern usage, and in an older tradition derived from the church fathers, when Thomas thinks of prayer he has in mind that much narrower practice, as we call it, of "petitionary" prayer, that is, the practice of asking God for what we want.[9] And this is not just his primary word for it. He takes for granted that asking God for things is, and should be, our principal practice of conversation with God. It is not, as he reminds us, that God doesn't know our needs anyway so that we have to inform him of them, for our Father in heaven knows all our needs well ahead of us. It is rather we who need in prayer to set our wants and desires before God honestly and truthfully just as we experience them, no matter what they are, so that by means of that prayer our Father in heaven can read our needs back to us, interpret them for us. For, Thomas says, "Oratio est quodammodo interpretativa voluntatis humanae," that is, "Prayer is in a certain manner an interpretation of what we human beings want."[10]

That is the reason why, though God does not need our prayers, we certainly do: for we do not always know what we want, our desires are complicated, "*plicata*," he says, crumpled up, folded over onto one another, so that we do not recognize what they truly are and for that reason cannot own them. Therefore, we have to unfold them, "explicate" them, in the only way possible to us, just as we are, that is, confused and befuddled even as to what desire we are there expressing. That is the way of honest prayer. Because we do not know what we really want, we can only place our desires before God exactly as we experience them so that God can read them back to us, *ut eas impleat*, Thomas says, that is, so that our Father in heaven may read back to us our truest desires and fulfill them. Thus, in prayer, our desires are at once honestly expressed just as they are and without pious pretense, and at the same time those desires are interpreted, *explicata*, as to what they really mean. For not by any means are what we think we want and what we truly want always the same. We all know that, being prone to passive self-ignorance at the best, and at the worst to active self-deception.

In this way Thomas shares none of that squeamishness about petitionary prayer that one hears sometimes indulged by very high-minded people, as if there were something mean, spiritually immature, small-minded, and excessively needy about asking God to meet our petty desires and wants, and as if spiritually grown-up people will pray only that God's will be done come what may. Strange it is how such mature Christians neglect the rather grubbier practice, also recommended by Jesus, of asking our Father in heaven for daily supplies of bread. Sophisticated prayer, Jesus tells us, is for Pharisees, who like to be heard standing up before an audience and in loud voices informing God of their disinterested desires and evidently expecting encouraging pats on the back for their adult high-mindedness. The publican, by contrast, being a sinner, hides away and simply groans. He is needy and though no doubt ashamed of his needs prays desperately out of them. He knows being in need is all he has got to offer.

THE PRAYER OF JESUS

But groaning, Thomas says, is not just for sinners. Did Jesus pray, he asks, *secundum suam sensualitatem?*[11] The Latin phrase is hard to translate, but the question means something like "Did Jesus pray out of (or perhaps "in accordance with") his animal desires?" and, in character, Thomas answers that it depends what you mean. Jesus in the Garden of Gethsemane "began to be greatly distressed and troubled," Mark tells us. He "fell to the ground"—this reads like the narrative of an eyewitness, and the tradition is that Mark as a very young man or boy was there at the time and witnessed Jesus's distress. And then Jesus prayed, and by all accounts very bluntly too, for the grammatical mood is not deprecating and conditional, it is an unconditional imperative, the plea of a troubled man, a man in pain: "Father, for you all things are possible: remove this cup from me," as if to say, "Father, you are free to will it. Do so will."

Of course, you will say, there is more to it than that cry of desperation, for Mark's account adds that Jesus said: "Yet not what I will, rather what you will." But the addendum is otiose. Mark's Jesus is no stoic.[12] You do not need the additional phrase, because it simply glosses the pleading as having been placed before his Father, God, that is, it glosses it as a prayer, and that rather goes without saying, since the address to his Father is already there in the pleading. In short, Jesus's words place his animal need before God, and that is what makes his fear to be his prayer. That is the reason, Thomas says, why Jesus is shown as praying *secundum suam sensualitatem*, he makes a prayer out of his animal self. It is "for our instruction ... [that Jesus] wanted us to know what in his natural human will he desired, and to what his animal impulses drew him."[13] But it is important not to get this wrong. To say that Jesus "prays for our instruction" is not to say that he does not really pray in distress but only pretends to. His distress is real, and, Thomas says, it "shows us that it is permitted for human beings out of their natural desires to will something other than what God wills." And then he adds the authority of Augustine in support of what he knows to be for some, perhaps especially for those spiritual sophisticates, a surprisingly raw, unprocessed, and unspiritual thought. For Augustine says it was in this way that Christ, bearing the weight of his humanity, shows that he has a human will of his own; and in accordance with that human will he prays "Take this chalice away from me." But because he wished to be a righteous man and to be moved back toward God, he adds, "Not, though, as I wish it, but rather as you do," which is as if to say [to us]: "See yourself in me: and you will see that it is quite acceptable to pray for what you wish even though God may wish otherwise."

Jesus, at least, prayed honestly as any human would. Indeed, you could say that his honesty before God was his prayer. At any rate, so say Thomas and Augustine.[14]

Such honesty can make us uneasy. Fake piety is easier than such un-processed neediness. And there is something humanly truthful about the prayer of Jesus in Gethsemane as Mark recalls it. But that realism itself pales before Mark's account of the even starker fear expressed in Jesus's last words on the cross. There is a disconcerting pathos about Mark's dying Jesus, for if he trusts his Father he does so without reassurance, and not only because of his physical pain, though there is in him none of the magisterial calm that Luke and John report; nor is it only because he has been abandoned by men, above all by his friends. It is because he fears the ultimate disaster and seems to experience it—that he has been abandoned even by his Father. "My God, my God, why have you forsaken me?" he cries. And he dies, his question falling upon deaf ears as it would seem, for in Mark's gospel it is left unanswered. Luke tells us that in Gethsemane an angel was sent to Jesus to console him. No such encouragement is offered here in Mark's narrative as death beckons, no inspiring last words heroically evoked, just a "loud cry" and then a dead and empty silence. As I understand it, the original version of Mark's Gospel ended with another emptiness, that of the tomb, the Resurrection narrative being later tacked on by another hand, as if the bleakness of this downbeat ending was, as it stood, too much to bear.

At all events, even as Mark's narrative now reads, if Jesus's prayer in the Garden teaches tough lessons, Jesus's prayer on the cross might seem to be little short of blasphemous. But for all that it might seem to be the despairing cry of a wretched man who has lost faith in his Father's will, it isn't. However bleak and needy, it's still a prayer to his God, indeed it is a further, yet more radical, model of how to pray, offered, once more Thomas says, "for our instruction." Certainly it is stronger meat, as ways of praying go, than the resigned calm of Luke's "Father, into your hands I commend my spirit." And just as surely Mark's narrative requires us to adjust our notions of what good praying looks like, only this time the adjustment needed is more disturbing still. Surprisingly it was the centurion standing by who somehow understood what had just happened: "Truly this man was the Son of God," he said, it seems on the evidence alone of those desperate last words of a humiliated Christ. That is pretty smart theology for a conscripted corporal in the Roman army.

PRAYER AND THE TRINITY

So where is Thomas with all this? And what has it to do with those formal, and professorial, questions of second-order theological epistemology that I raised just now, with the rational proofs of the existence of God, with the dauntingly technical speculative theology of the Trinity, with that severely negative theology, with that trope of the "darkness of God"? The connection lies in the nature of that prayer of Christ in which is shown why, when Christians, at any rate Catholics, Roman or otherwise, invoke the Trinity in their lives, they pray "in the name of the Father and of the Son and of the Holy Spirit," and as they do so make the sign of the cross. When they do this it is as if to say: it is true, as even the philosophers know, that, God not being any kind of thing, we are drawn even by reason into God's impenetrable cloud of unknowing; it is true that the same darkness of God is deepened by the very demonstration of God's existence, which, far from placing God within the grasping hands of reason, shows that in their highest powers of reason human beings are drawn even more deeply and surely into the divine darkness; and it is true that by the revelation of the mystery of the godhead they are drawn into the Trinitarian being itself, and so into some share in how God knows and loves himself; yet there too they are drawn into a mystery that is, in itself, utterly beyond human powers to understand. As we grapple with those overlapping and ever deepening mysteries of reason and of faith, the best that can be done with it all is to ask the theologians to spell out and articulate, as does Thomas in his *Summa,* some formal, speculative propositions with which they can, as it were within a framework, stabilize our many sorts of discourse about God. But when Christians want to read the Trinity within their lives, or better, when they want their lives to be read within and by the Trinitarian life, there they truly enter by way of all knowledge and desire into the darkness of God mapped onto our human ground, within their sight. Then it is that they make the sign of the cross. Then it is that they enter into the true darkness of God, God's own darkness in the person of the crucified Son.

For the cross is what the Trinity looks like when it becomes visible within human history, and it appears only that way because of our sin. Jesus's desolation in his passion and death wreaks havoc with our natural expectations of how a God should appear among us, for on the cross is no superhuman, but one "despised," and as one seeming to be, in the words of Isaiah, "the most rejected of men."[15] Here is no theoretical unknowing, for here on the cross the godhead is not recognizable even as a man, never mind as a God. But that is how things stand for the theologians, they have to work with what is there in the darkness of God thus revealed, or not at all. For Jesus's prayer in the Garden of Gethsemane and on Golgotha is where the Trinity is inscribed within time, history, and human experience, inscribed upon our sensual, animal being. Jesus's last words are the broken prayers of a man who can address his Father only *secundum . . . sensualitatem.* Here, then, finally is discovered the concrete and lived meaning of the darkness of God, now no longer as a metatheology, but as an event that falls within the narrative grasp of first-order experience; the darkness of God is now the Trinity come among us and palpable as an animal's pain. Herein lies the mystical, the *mysterium fidei* that is within the human grasp to be lived. And I suppose we should be taken aback that if, as Thomas said, the mystery of the inner life of the Godhead has only one way of appearing among us, namely "in its effects" in history and time, then on such an account that Trinitarian life is known to us in and by way of the death throes of a man falsely judged criminal by some very religious people not unlike ourselves. But that is what the world is thereby revealed to be, and that is why we have been taught to make the sign of the cross when we call upon the Trinity in prayer. The Trinity and the cross map on to one another like a palimpsest of transparencies superimposed the one upon the other: either way you have to read through the one to read the other. "Surely this man was the Son of God," says the Roman mercenary, getting it: surely the mystery of the Godhead is made present to us, at last, on the cross.

THREE

Reason, the Eucharist, and the Body

WHAT I GOT WRONG

In this paper I propose a theological defense of human reason, contentious as in our times such a proposal is. More precisely, I will explain why it is important not only philosophically but also theologically and as a matter of faith to defend the power of human reason to know of God's existence, the same God that, under other descriptions, is known only by faith. I take it to be the view of Thomas Aquinas that this is so, and it is broadly a reading of his account of the relation between faith and reason that I wish to defend here.

I once said in a book that a second, and, as I then thought, connected proposition, could be defended, if only programmatically, one invoking a stronger warrant for this same case of Thomas's, namely that his view of faith as entailing God's rational demonstrability was endorsed in a dogmatic decree of the first Vatican Council of 1870–72.[1] This decree, I said then, expressed the church's unqualified confidence in the power of human reason to know God, at least in principle, declaring—rather drastically, it will be thought—those persons to be anathematized who (in Norman Tanner's translation) deny "that the one true God, our creator and lord, can ... be known with certainty from the things that have been made, by the natural light of reason."[2] The decree seemed to me then to say that reason, in its characteristic exercise of proof, can by its own unaided power know our Creator and Lord God to exist, that same God we address when we pray, the same God whose Word was incarnate in the man Jesus, the same God who forgives us through the church's power of reconciliation, the same God whose grace is the cause of our sanctification. And in that book I attempted to make both cases, namely that the church at Vatican I had in mind declaring dogmatically and as a matter of faith what Thomas taught as a theologian and *in propria persona*.

For the sake of clarity a third proposition needs to be distinguished from either of the above, namely that there are valid and sound proofs of the existence of God to be had, and that Thomas Aquinas provides them by way of five rational arguments. I do not recall ever maintaining the view that if it is a matter of faith that the existence of God is demonstrable by reason it follows that any known argument for God is thus authoritatively endorsed. Stronger still than that should the grounds for practical skepticism be, since perhaps there is in fact no known rational argument that conclusively demonstrates God's existence, and maybe there never will be; and finally, there is the simple and plain fact that, even were there to be conclusive rational proofs of God's existence it is most unlikely, as Thomas himself makes clear, that everybody, or even most people, are going to be convinced by them[3]—though that is neither here nor there to his point, for validity is a matter of logic; being convincing, on the other hand, is an entirely different matter of rhetoric and of psychology.

All that uncertainty notwithstanding, there is, I thought, no inconsistency in maintaining that there must be some such rational demonstration of God's existence, even if none is currently known or if none ever will be. You could have known in 1637 that Fermat's last theorem was capable of being proved even though no successful proof of it was forthcoming until Andrew Wiles showed how to do it in Cambridge University in 1993; and more generally there are well-known mathematical procedures for proving the provability of a theorem even when these proofs are not themselves proofs of the theorem. Just so in the theological case: it is consistent to say that it must be possible to do it even if no one has certainly done it. And thereby you say something important about theology, as also something theologically important.

In summary, then, in my book I argued first that Thomas Aquinas believed it to be a matter of faith that God's existence is rationally demonstrable by means of formal proof; second, I took it that Vatican I authoritatively and intentionally endorsed Thomas's opinion on the matter; and third, I argued that the first two propositions could be defended even were no actual arguments for God's existence known conclusively to be valid and sound.

Alas for my opinion on these matters, no less an authority than Fergus Kerr quickly assured me that I was wrong as to the second of these three propositions, because whatever was to be said as to the correctness or otherwise of my reading of Thomas, I was at least wrong in supposing that the decree of Vatican I had anything to do with supporting him on any account whatsoever.[4] The bishops at Vatican I, he said, had other fish to fry than defending Thomas Aquinas as to the formal provability of God's existence; still less, of course, did the Council have in mind defending Thomas's actual proofs—the "five ways," as they are known. More to the point, Kerr shows that in affirming that God's existence can "with certainty be known by the natural light of reason" Vatican I need not have had in mind, and on the evidence did not have in mind, anything like formally valid and sound rational proof, what Thomas calls *probatio*.[5] Herewith I concede all three points. Historians will know what the bishops at Vatican I had in mind to anathematize, and I do not; and Kerr shows that I got it wrong in supposing that they had Thomas Aquinas in mind at all, whether in his general conviction that God's existence is rationally demonstrable or more specifically in support of the proposition that the five ways pull off proofs with validity and soundness.

This seems conclusive as to what Vatican I requires by way of reason's power to know God: just don't deny that human reason can, by some means or other unaided, get there. The much stronger case that I made in *Faith, Reason and the Existence of God* was in that narrow connection naive and historically ill informed, as I am happy to concede. No matter: hereby I eschew the Vatican Council's support and stick to the still contentious and much-contended reading of Thomas according to which the existence of

God is demonstrable by reason alone, and that it was considerations of faith that held him to that account of reason's power to know God. Deny what you like as to the validity of any known proofs, Thomas's included, but to deny in principle the possibility of a proof of God on grounds of faith is, I shall say he thinks, to get something importantly wrong about reason, and in consequence to get other things importantly wrong about faith. That is the case, narrower than before, that I now make in this chapter. It is controversial enough even thus narrowed.

REASON IN ITS MINIMAL CAPACITY

Such preliminary throat-clearing out of the way, there are two kinds of theological argument supportive of a role for reason in theology, the first being, as I call it, of a minimalist sort and negative, the second more robust and positive, and as I shall say maximalist. But might I first step back from those principal concerns and offer a generalization about reason by way of appeal to a medieval philosophical truism? It is a truism you find Thomas Aquinas sometimes appealing to, though in fact he and others got it from their Latin translation of Aristotle's *Peri hermeneias.* "Eadem est scientia oppositorum," Thomas says—One and the same is the knowledge of contraries.[6] You might paraphrase one implication of this truism by saying that a basic notion of reason seems to be connected with procedures for first defining and then settling disagreements, since you can get worthwhile disagreements going only where there is agreed common ground to contest: then as between you and your opponent there is a *differentia.* Where you don't agree, or can't, as to what you are disagreeing about, where there is no *eadem scientia,* you have but heterogeneity, or as medieval philosophers called it, a *diversitas;* that is, you get but cross-purposes— as we can disagree about whether this object is red or green, but we don't exactly disagree if you say it is green and I say that it is six foot long; or, to take a medieval example, medieval theologians thought of heretics, whether of the Christian variety, or Muslim or Jewish, as belonging to a common family of disagreement, since with them you knew what you were disagreeing about—the falling-out was within the family, as it were—

whereas they would mostly have been simply puzzled by Buddhists, hardly knowing where to start with them.

That said, let me put in very blunt terms the minimalist proposition about reason in theology that I have in mind to defend, namely that reason has procedures on offer to do with the business of identifying and then settling disagreements, as distinct from diversities. You may disagree with all sorts of substantive propositions about reason that Thomas comes up with, but if you can do so such that there are procedures for settling such disagreements that you can agree upon, then after all you and Thomas do agree to that extent as to what reason is and as to what it demands of you thus far. For at least as to *that* you and he agree about wherein lies the common territory of your disagreement. And if that is so, will he not have drawn you into rational contestation with him in two moves, if not in one?

There are perhaps those who would want to dismiss so formal and dialectical a ploy in the following way. Thomas thinks it is a matter of faith that the existence of God is demonstrable by reason alone, and that if you understand the act of faith correctly you will understand why. But even though theologians today are much better disposed toward Thomas than they used to be in the early to mid-twentieth century, there is hardly one among them of whatever theological tradition who thinks he is right on that score,[7] preferring on the whole the proposition that, on the contrary, it is essential to the defense of faith that the existence of God be shown to be absolutely beyond the reach of rational demonstration. There are all sorts of grounds offered, Kantian and non-Kantian, for the theologians' reluctance to share Thomas's optimism about what Kant called "speculative" reason and its limits, but one of the most commonly put, and as casually as commonly, is neo-Pascalian. You still hear it said that even if it were philosophically possible it's simply no use for a theologian to try to prove the existence of God on rational grounds, because any God you could prove the existence of by purely rational means would be, as Pascal so famously put it, a God "of the philosophers," and a God of the philosophers could not be the same God as the God "of Abraham, Isaac and Jacob," the God of faith.

Hearing this sort of case from a good Barthian theologian would not be surprising. More so is to get a reading of Thomas himself, such as that of Fergus Kerr, according to which even if a rational proof that God exists could be had—and he implies that Thomas isn't really serious in supposing that it can be—the "God exists" of the philosopher could not mean the same as the "God exists" of Christian faith.[8] Here there is no historical question, but an issue that is systematic and philosophical, for Kerr believes it follows that rational proof of God, even if successful, wouldn't get you to the same God as the God of Christian faith. But this appears to be a non sequitur.

For I cannot see Thomas Aquinas being much disconcerted by the nonequivalence of the divine names, philosophy proving God under one description, faith believing under another, and Thomas knows perfectly well that none of the descriptions under which he thinks God's existence is proved—"prime mover," "first cause," "necessary being" and so forth— mean the same as "Father, Son and Holy Spirit." After all, he knows that even as concerns the rational proofs themselves, "prime mover," "first cause," and "necessary being" don't mean the same as each other, but he would have been surprised to know of this being considered an objection. Just because two descriptions do not mean the same, it doesn't follow that they are not descriptions of the same identical thing, just as "the square of 1" and "the square root of 1" do not mean the same, though the value both formulas yield is 1; or, as John Haldane has put it, just because "blockage in the system" and "a small piece of masonry" do not mean the same it does not follow that what's blocking the system isn't a small piece of masonry.[9] Just so here: you would of course still have to show that the "necessary being" known by reason is the same God as the cause and object of Trinitarian faith. But then Thomas puts in some 149 articles of close argument between the five ways and the opening of his discussion of the Trinity, purporting to show just that. When Thomas says at the end of each of his proofs, "et hoc omnes dicunt Deum," this should be translated not as "and this is how all people talk about God," because manifestly they don't commonly, if ever, talk about God as "prime mover," or "necessary being," and no one should imagine Thomas not knowing that—or even as "And this is what all people mean when they talk about God," since on the contrary hardly anybody but a few philosophers mean any such thing, and Thomas knows that too. The phrase is more properly translated as "And this is the [same] God [as] the one all people speak of," for example, when they pray, or make the sign of the cross, or whatever they do in practice of their faith; and though of course that is a proposition which itself needs some argument that you could dispute, there is no good reason for the theologians to take offense in principle, at any rate not on Pascal's grounds.

More telling, however, is the objection that Thomas's case about faith is simultaneously both outrageously overbearing in its claims to dictate to the philosophers' rational autonomy and, at the same time, riskily self-undermining. It is a provocation to the philosophers that theological authorities should appear to be telling them what they can and can't do, and on nonphilosophical grounds. But the theologians too will have cause to worry about the decree, because it would appear to place faith in thrall to what must in principle be a contestable philosophical proposition—for a proposition's being philosophical would seem to guarantee its contestability. Therefore, were the philosophers to succeed in showing that reason could not in principle show the existence of God, then any account of faith entailing that it could do so would fall with the success of the philosophers' counterarguments. For if what a proposition entails is false, then the proposition entailing it is false. But I do not think either fear is justified. The situation here in point of the decree's coherence is somewhat similar to another, just as hotly disputed, proposition which in a manner analogous connects matters of faith with what is epistemologically much less certain than rational argument, that is, with variably contingent secular fact.

Suppose you maintain—as I do, though I know there are some theologians who do not—first that faith in the resurrection of Jesus Christ entails his bodily resurrection, and second that bodily resurrection entails that one and the same body which hung on the cross has now ascended to the right hand of the Father; then you claim to know on grounds of faith that as a matter of contingent fact there are not going to be any preserved bones of Jesus's dead body lying somewhere to be discovered in the desert of Palestine. In short, you know that by early on the third day the tomb was empty. But whether the tomb was empty or not was a straightforward matter of witnesses' observation at the time, and of the truthfulness of their reporting; and the proposition that Jesus was raised on the third day is therefore of a defeasible kind. There is a general, but simple, point in logic at stake here. Of course if a proposition is true then necessarily factual claims to the contrary are false: so necessarily if it is true that Jesus's body was raised from the dead, then the tomb was empty. But that "necessarily" of faith's entailment does not make the tomb's being empty any less an empirical, factual claim. As Thomas says, so long as Socrates is sitting then necessarily the proposition "Socrates is sitting" is true. But it does not follow from this that Socrates's sitting is necessary; it remains a perfectly contingent matter of fact—he just has to stand up and walk away and the proposition "Socrates is sitting" becomes false.[10] And the position in point of the logic of the Resurrection is in like case: of necessity, if you believe in Jesus's bodily resurrection then you claim to know that as a matter of fact the tomb was empty. It does not follow that the tomb's being empty is a necessary truth. Hence, had it not been empty, had Jesus's body been there all the time and the witnesses lying, or had it been spirited away by the disciples and hidden elsewhere, then belief in the resurrection of Jesus would have become unsustainable. Logically the counterfactual remains available: it could have been true, even if we know on grounds of faith that it is false.

I could therefore see why some theologians would worry about faith's being tied in with a historically contingent entailment of this kind were it being maintained that a Resurrection faith's meaning is reducible to the factual consequence it entails—as if, as the late bishop of Durham David Jenkins used to put it, it would follow that such belief in the Resurrection would amount to nothing more than a story about "a bag of bones." But it is hard to know what is going on when one hears Christian theologians worrying in this sort of way. After all, every time they recite their creed they declare what in faith is true. And among the truths the Creed declares to be of faith are some obviously plain, nontheological, historical facts, namely that Jesus was "crucified, died and was buried." Were those contingent historical assertions not true, Christian faith would be in vain. So says the Creed. I therefore cannot see why theologians should want to box themselves into so conceptually tight a corner as they do if they insist that were your faith to entail factual consequences it would be reduced to those consequences. Nothing of the sort follows. You can with perfect consistency say first, that Resurrection faith depends upon a certain historical fact's being the case, namely that the tomb was empty, and, second, that faith in the Resurrection could not consist in just that fact's being the case. For the hypothetical proposition "If belief in the resurrection of Jesus is true then the tomb was empty" is not of course convertible with the proposition, "If the tomb was empty then belief in the Resurrection is true."[11] Of course, then, Resurrection faith consists in more than belief in a mere historical fact, even if its truth entails one.

For such reasons I concede that these matters merely of logic say nothing at all of interest about that Resurrection faith itself. But being interesting about the Resurrection was not the point, which was only to illustrate a parallel and more general point, and equally one in mere logic, about faith's authority and reason's autonomy. In the same way as to say that belief in the resurrection of Jesus entails a certain empirical fact's being true does not rob that fact of its empirical, contingent character, so to say that faith's authority dictates that a certain philosophical proposition is true is not to rob faith of its certainty by virtue of thus linking it to a contestable truth claim, nor is the assertion of that linkage to a philosophical proposition to reduce faith to the epistemological level of a philosophical claim. So Thomas's case for faith's authority does nothing to rob reason of its autonomy. On the contrary, faith's certainty concedes that autonomy to reason. For if by faith we know that reason is capable of knowing God, then it would seem to follow that reason can by itself know that it is capable of knowing God—in the same way that knowing without proof that $2 + 2 = 4$ does not deprive the mathematician of the benefits of Russell and Whitehead's *Principia Mathematica,* which shows what is formally required of a proof that it is so. And as in the one case so in the other: the existence of God would remain to be shown by a philosophically sound and logically valid proof, and it takes a philosopher to know whether or not you have got one. So all the work of reason remains to be done by reason itself and of its own resources. None of its work is done for it by faith.

Neither does it follow, just because faith entails that reason is capable of knowing of its own power to know God, that this leaves faith vulnerable to refutation by mere philosophers' arguments, such as Kant's. To the contrary—for if you know with the certainty of faith that Kant is wrong to deny that speculative reason can know God, then you know that Kant is wrong *simpliciter*: but even then, you still have to show by philosophical argument that he is wrong, and very possibly you will fail to do so. Nor does that mean that faith depends subjectively on actually producing a knockdown proof of God's existence. It certainly does not depend upon Thomas's own five ways having to be counted on as valid proofs of God.

It just requires that you do not so construe faith objectively as to entail the impossibility of rational proof in principle.

Even more surely, you do not yourself have to be personally able to refute Kant philosophically if you are to be certain of your faith. In fact, quite obviously, you can have the firmest faith possible without having the least notion that Kant denied one of its entailments. Better still than that, there is a blessed majority of faithful believers who haven't the faintest idea that there ever was an eighteenth-century German philosopher named Kant at all, such is the happy life for some. So it would seem that you can eat your cake and have it, and that the merit of Thomas's position is that it allows consistently both for reason's autonomy in action and for faith's authority in principle. And, prima facie, that would seem to be a motive for taking Thomas's position a bit more seriously than theologians commonly do.

POSTMODERNISM

Except that the postmodernists won't let them. Let us just for a moment recap. My case is that either all is heterogeneity and there is no argument to be had about God's existence, or else there are some arguments to be had—but that, if there are arguments to be had, then this can only be across a common territory of dispute. Thus by way of this "minimal" account of reason we can say that it consists in the territory occupied in common by opposed beliefs such that they contest with one another over it. But the postmodernists will tell the theologians that there is no such territory for reason to occupy, that reason, as offering any overarching narrative, whether of contestation or of comparison, is a myth of the Enlightenment and of Western modernity. And a good number of theologians and students of religion of my acquaintance have bought into this story, maintaining that it is indeed true that all is heterogeneity, or as the medieval philosophers said, *diversitas*, or, as Jacques Derrida says, "Every other is every [bit] other"—as one might say, in one way or another "the other" reigns supreme. And they propose to conduct their respective businesses on those terms of the priority of otherness, rather than on any of a pretentiously universalistic kind.[12] Nothing overarches, least of all reason, which, as understood within the rationalisms of modernity, constructs relations of otherness only on the basis of a primary and absolutely primordial sameness.

Of course the nose twitches in suspicion at a critique of grand narratives that is itself rooted in as grand a narrative of intellectual history as one could imagine, consisting as it does in a historically unsatisfying construal of grand epochs of that history into the pre- and the postmodern, with a sort of mythological modernity set in the middle as a point of contrast with both. But what is crucial to this critique of modernity is the critique of its rationalism, as a totalizing and hegemony-claiming, plurality-denying conspiracy, no doubt phallocentric and neocolonialist to boot, on behalf of sameness and identity. Fair enough: for all I know modernist rationality is all of these things, and certainly no theologian is going to bow before a petty godlet that is the idolatrous product of a reason so conceived—not Thomas, not I.

In view of which could I make my meaning plain: the case for revisiting Thomas's quite drastically minimalist account of reason owes nothing much to what theologians or cultural theorists defend as modernist when they do, or to what they reject, as today more do in the name of the postmodern. It owes little either to the so-called metaphysical God of Enlightenment theodicies or to the postmetaphysical God, whether of a John Caputo or a Jean-Luc Marion. Hence it neither stakes claims to a pretentiously universalistic, overarching, and *given* normativity of reason in respect of religious belief claims nor makes concessions to its mirror-image deregulated pluralisms. Rather, it tells you of a plague to be visited upon both houses of the a priori: it tells you to explore how differences themselves differ, neither in order to collapse them into some higher, universal, modernist rational sameness nor to dissolve them into some postmodern thesis that the only ultimate is the penultimate, but in order to discover the common ground you differ over, the *eadem scientia* you are drawn into precisely by the *oppositio*.

To give but one kind of example: you can't know a priori whether a Christian's saying God is a trinity of persons, and a Jew or a Muslim's saying God is one, is like saying God is red, not blue, a true *oppositio*, or whether it is more like saying God is red, not six foot long, a *diversitas*; or whether it is neither because the language of God passes beyond any language of differentiation, even of complete differentiation.

In truth, before God the language of difference begins to swallow itself up, like the snake its tail: for "complete difference" is a nonsense phrase, an oxymoron. If there is difference then it is in a respect; if there is difference in every respect then there is no calculable difference at all, for the language of difference has migrated off any semantic map capable of describing it. And that is why Derrida's "Tout autre est tout autre" is but a form of higher nonsense, a species of unmeaning, if grandiloquent, bombast. Better than Derrida is what negative theologians all actually say, Jewish, Christian, or Muslim, agreeing, sometimes in other terms, with Nicholas of Cusa, that God is the one and only being that is *non-aliud*, "not-other," escaping every discourse, whether of sameness, difference, or diversity, so that as of God "otherness" cannot come into it at all, and the apophatic nature of this description is not to be confused with the plain nonsense of the "completely other," as in Derrida. Nor, then, and by the same token, can "sameness." That being the case, how otherwise than within their shared constructions of unknowing may the theologians of the Abrahamic world faiths understand their differences in the matter of the oneness of God and the Trinity of persons? Is it not the case that theologians of all three traditions, being in the same way constrained to conclude that all theology ends with the defeat of the very categories of otherness and sameness, that before God otherness as such collapses hand in hand with sameness? And, that being so, does not counting fail us too, whether of one or three? For counting depends upon the identifications of "this" other than "that," which also has become demonstrably impossible as of God. So Jews, Christians, and Muslims just have to work it out whether they do or they don't disagree about the construction of that divine transcendence; and what they are exercising in that working out, in the very possibility of a conversation between them, is a sort of minimal, but still normative, conception of reason, an *eadem scientia*.

Hence, when Thomas maintains that theology is *argumentativa*, he means that it is in this way exploratory of the *sic et non*, the "for and against," of faith.[13] And this minimalist account of reason is just that which is discovered in the course of exploring the possibilities of theological argument, and, so far as that minimalism goes, is not much more than that. Does not faith have to concede at least that much? It is hard to see how any articulated faith could concede less than that to reason, to reasoning, in this its minimal sense.

Sketchy enough as it is, then, that is as much as I will say in defense of the first of those two subsidiary propositions about reason, and I will pass on to the second. For there is of course more to reason on Thomas's account than that minimal conception, a richer, more complex, conception of it than any that has been available to us among the theologians and philosophers since his time; but it is also one without which it is impossible to understand his case for the possibility of a rational proof of God. And I want now to suggest that if we are to recapture something of what he has to offer here we could do well to start elsewhere than among the theologians and cultural theorists of our times and would do better to look specifically among the arts, but especially to poetry and music.

REASON IN ITS MAXIMAL SENSE

But you will have to forgive me if, art being long and life short, I give you little more than heads of an argument, an outline for an argument-strategy, as it were. First, let us dispose of an instinctive though often unarticulated prejudice against any conception of reason beyond that of its minimal deployment, for that prejudice can get in the way of our reading Thomas properly. As there are cultural theorists so there are theologians who just don't seem to like reason very much. It seems so unfriendly to feeling for a start, and its universalizations seem to them inadequate to the rich complexity of life more generally. And one has to concede that reason reduced to the minimal sense, as formal ratiocination, is a dull, flat, and thus far not very profitable thing. And you might correspondingly be uninspired, as many are, by how far Thomas's essential definition (as he calls it) of a human being as a "rational animal" limps so laggardly behind the living, complex, vibrant, carnal reality of any actual human being.[14] And while it is true that Thomas is no enemy of reason in that narrow sense of reasoning, he is equally clear that you cannot get the role of reason in theology right, even in that limited employment of it which is ratiocination, until you place it within a far wider understanding of what it is for a human being to be a rational animal than any which might be deduced exclusively from a rationality so minimally conceived.

Though Thomas doesn't quite put it this way himself, my suggestion is that you get the hang of the hot, full-blooded, and scarlet thing that he means by "rational animal" if you can see how of all the activities in which human beings engage, music making best exemplifies how animals can be rational, that is to say, human; and I will first say a few things by way of explanation of that. And then I will say that you can see why this should be so in his theology of the Eucharist. There you can grasp a sort of ideal type, an exemplary case, of what rationality means to Thomas, and there you can see why he might think that reason, in that sense in which music is typically rational, has a sort of Eucharistic, or perhaps more broadly a sacramental, shape, epistemologically speaking. And then I shall say that a proof of the existence of God is just a case of reason in its minimal expression as ratiocination fulfilling itself in the same sort of epistemological shape that music and the Eucharist have. But take all of them together, poetry, music, sacrament, and proof, and you have what Thomas means by reason in its most general and fundamental sense, its "maximal" sense, as I shall call it.

POETRY, MUSIC, AND REASON

To understand this maximal sense the first step is to begin where Thomas does, placing us humans where we belong in the big scheme of things, that is to say, with the proposition that we humans are generically animals. Therefore, whatever we humans do we do it as animals do it.[15] If we love, we love as animals do, and if my cat cannot reciprocate on equal terms the affection I bestow upon her this is not because she is an animal and I am not, it is because I am, and she is not, a *rational* animal. If we suffer, we suffer as animals do, we both get headaches; if I know and love God, then I know and love God as only a being who gets headaches can, and if my cat cannot know and love God this again is not because my cat is an animal and I am not but because the cat is a different sort of animal from me: one might say that for Thomas I am a more fully realized animal, more fully animal-like, than my cat is. So, from one point of view my character as an animal contrasts with a brute's only in that mine is rational and the brute's is not, and beyond that it does not contrast at all.[16]

But then for Thomas my rationality places my nature in another point of contrast, that is, with angels. For if it is true that not all animals are rational, it is also true that nothing is rational except an animal. Angels know many more things than humans do but are not rational; God knows everything knowable, but not as humans do, not rationally. When it comes to how to know things, some animals, but only they, ratiocinate, for you need to have an animal body to think discursively, and for the same reason their communication is linguistic, structured by grammar and syntax; and that, as one of Thomas's earliest followers, Dante Alighieri, says, is what it is to be human. It's for that reason, as he puts it, that all forms of failure to be human consist in, or at least in some way show up in, failures of language.[17]

So a Dantean way of placing human beings is to say that only rational animals have meaningful bodies,[18] bodies that bear and transact meanings, bodies that "speak." Some have a problem with this, but they should think about how a smile speaks,[19] and of how Beatrice's smiles in *Paradiso* speak to the Dante in the poem. Or they might consider how "a man may smile, and smile, and be a villain," his smile saying one thing, his villainy another. Or think of the complexity of communication contained in that other famously ironic act which speaks, the kiss of Judas, that greeting of friends whereby he betrays Jesus: "Do you betray the Son of Man with [of all things] a kiss?" says Jesus, bitterly protesting at a cruel irony. To have a problem with how a smile or a kiss or a laugh can speak, thinking them to be somehow more material than formal language, is to be in danger of being generally misled about language: for it will be no easier to explain how formal speech speaks, conveys meaning. How less material than gestures of a hand or face are written alphabetical squiggles on a page bearing meaning? How are the vibrations of the larynx any less material than the *rictus* of the lips, either being expressive, sometimes, of the most profound thoughts? Some have a general problem about how meanings get into matter. But if that is so, their problem about meaning and formal language is no more nor less difficult of solution than how it is that a smile, or a kiss, or a laugh, can be the bearer of ironics. All are bits of body that say things. It is possible to explain the one only by such means as explain both.

Such, at any rate, is the view of Thomas Aquinas—it is from Thomas that Dante gets the idea: a rational animal is a meaning-bearing, sign-conveying lump of organized sensuous matter, and we call those human bits of matter "bodies" for the very reason that they are matter alive with that form of life which consists in the transactions of meaning—they are alive precisely as communicating, and their quality of life is in the quality of their acts of communication. A rational animal is speaking matter, it is a body in its character as language. So back to language, and, to help us out there, back to Judas's kiss. You can grasp the terrible irony of that kiss because you grasp how its twofold meanings contradict one another: what Judas's kiss says as conventional sign—the greeting of friends—is subverted by what is said by his doing it—betraying his savior and Lord. It's not of course a unique case: think of the performatively contradictory behavior of parents who smack their child in order to teach it not to solve problems by means of violence. The very smack itself unsays the correction.

That is step one: utterances perform something, we say, and, as we might add, signs can effect, as to say the words "I promise" *is*, under certain conditions, to promise and thereby to make an undertaking to be held to what one has said.[20] But also performances utter, that is to say the very materiality of the signifier itself can bear its own meaning. That is part of what is meant by saying that humans are rational in Thomas's sense, namely that human bodies signify, or rather, some matter is a human body precisely insofar as it signifies. You might say that brute animal bodies signal things like their pain or pleasure but don't signify either, for they lack the required vocabularies and discourses. Angels don't have bodies, so as Dante says, if they transact meanings, it is not by means of language that they do so, which is the same as to say that they are not rational. And that is step two.

To take step three, consider poetry. Herbert McCabe once said that "poetry is language trying to be bodily experience,"[21] and that seems right, except for the "trying to be." Poetic meanings work through a complex set of transactions between what is conveyed by the meaning of the words considered as formal speech and what is conveyed by the signifier in its material, physical character as shape on the page or as sound uttered. Think of the difference inflection makes between saying "Emma Kirkby is not just a pretty *voice*" and "Emma Kirkby is not just a *pretty* voice"—here it is the words' music, their inflection, which delivers the difference of meaning,[22] not the words as abstract verbal signs, for the words, minus the vocal inflection, are in either case identical. Poetry is the meal made of such material tonal devices in a sort of contrapuntal interweaving of verbal and tonal meanings. As Oliver Davies puts it, in poetry the signifier itself is "foregrounded,"[23] so that the total work of meaning is carried not alone by the formal meanings of the words but also by that meaning which is conveyed by the material, aural, qualities of the speech acts themselves, the rhythmic speech patterns, assonance, inflection, and so forth, these two in their contrapuntal interplay. That is poetry being the body. It doesn't have to "try" to be one—in fact it might have been better had Herbert said that it is music that poetry is "trying to be."

Which is to the point. For then Herbert added: "And music is bodily experience trying to be language,"[24] which again seems right except for the "trying to be." For if in poetry there is a contrapuntal weaving of the verbally signified with the signifier itself, in whose materiality of being uttered there is also an utterance, in music the signifier in its materiality is so absolutely foregrounded that all is reduced to it, with nothing left to it in the character of verbal language at all,[25] for music is all rhythm and pitch and melody and harmony and dissonance. To see the difference between the verbal and the musical, therefore, think of this: when I say, "The cat is on the mat," you can attend to the meaning exclusively, so that the sounds disappear, absorbed entirely into the meaning, you hear the sounds as something said, as words structured syntactically; or you can, if you try hard enough, attend to the mere noise of the utterance, the meaning disappearing into it, you hear the words simply as sounds, just as one would hear words uttered in an entirely unfamiliar foreign language.[26] But either way there is a distinction between the meaning of the words as words, and the performance of the words as sounds, there is a surplus physicality of sound that you can identify separately from the meaning. And even in poetry, the most nearly musical of all the verbal arts, the musicality of the sound can work its effect only in conjunction with formal verbal meaning.[27] But in music you cannot make an equivalent distinction, nor ought you to try. Music as such has no verbal meaning at all.[28] What you hear is what you get, meaning as sound, sound as meaning. In music there is no surplus, whether of physicality over and above the signifying sounds

themselves or of signification over and above those sounds and their struc-
turing in rhythm and pitch and melody and harmony. So you could say
that music is, like the Cheshire cat, all smile and no cat, because the matter
has disappeared into the meaning and the meaning has disappeared into
the matter. Music is matter entirely alive with meaning, at once the most
bodily and at the same time the most formal and abstract of human com-
munications.[29] And that is why I suggested that if you were Thomas you
might say (though he did not in fact say it) that music is the most rational
of human activities, for in music physicality and meaning, body and language, have become perfectly identified. Music is sound and fury signifying nothing that the sound and fury themselves do not signify. Music is all
body but precisely as language.[30] It is body entirely transparent to meaning. It is animality in its most transparent form as rationality. And that
was step four.

And now that we have got about as far as possible from what you
thought Thomas meant when I first used the word *rational* in this essay, I
can begin to explain what might truly be at stake when he talks about a rational knowledge of God. There is a fifth important step needed yet, but
on the way could I point in the right direction by hazarding a speculation:
the nearest you can get to a sort of spontaneous and demotic natural theology, to a sort of pretheological anticipation of theology, is in poetry and
in music, but especially in music. And if this is so, perhaps it is because of
those paradoxical conjunctions of music's being closest to us in the intense
physicality of our animal natures and yet wholly open as to its significance,
so very indeterminate, so lacking in particular reference, so purely formal,
and in that respect closest perhaps to arithmetic: and because of that formal character it opens up spaces of experience beyond our particularity,
beyond our confined individuality. Ancients did not think, as we do now,
of some music as sacred and some secular: historically that is a distinction
that Christians made first. Ancients thought music was sacred as such,
and whatever their reasons I think we moderns also intuitively experience
in all music a natural capacity for the transcendent, we can see it as a sort
of natural theurgy. And if that is so, it would appear to have to do with the
fact that music's very impersonality and otherness is what allows for such a
free, spontaneous, and utterly personal response. To paraphrase Nietzsche,
music is all feeling, but as subjectively and objectively "unhooked":[31] sub-

jectively unhooked, because it disengages from any one person's sadness or joy; and objectively unhooked, because its sadness or joy is not about anything in particular, it is feeling as anyone's, feeling that is at once absolutely selfless and absolutely objectless; for which reason it can be absolutely and entirely yours as well as absolutely and entirely anyone else's, always intensely individual and utterly transcending individuation, moving experience into a space free of the constative, or assertoric.[32] And perhaps that is why music is the most commonly experienced form of what medieval theologians called an *excessus*, or in Greek, *ekstasis*, or in English, "taking leave of your senses": but in music, by the most sensual, most bodily, of means.

MUSIC AND THE EUCHARIST

And that brings us to step five. And this is that music is, as I put it, "prototypically Eucharistic." And maybe by now it is possible to grasp the connective tissue of thoughts, the formal similarity of thought structure: for, on Thomas's account, in the Eucharist is brought to the absolute limit possible before our resurrection that same conjunction of absolute bodiliness and absolute transparency of meaning, for the Eucharist is a communication of the Word that is all body, and a body that is all communication, all word, all sign, and just insofar as it is all sign it is all matter, specifically edible matter. Or, and this is just another way Thomas has of putting the same, in the Eucharist there is nothing left of the bread and wine's materiality but only their character as signs, all smile and no cat again—there is, as he puts it, a "transubstantiation"—signs which make real a presence of Christ's body so that it pushes to the very limits any force we can lay hold of for the words *real* and *presence*. And then we have to add, "and beyond such limits." For the doctrine of the real presence of Christ in the Eucharist is, in Thomas, also a doctrine of the real absence.

We might say that it is in his teaching on the Eucharist that we find Thomas's last word on ontology, about what is most real. That ontology tells us that his paradigm of the real is the presence of Christ in the Eucharist, a bodily presence that is total communication, all word, but just on that account the more intensely bodily, not less. So, on the one hand, no body could be more present or more completely bodily than Christ's body as present in the Eucharist. For no body could be more purely language, word, matter as pure communication.

But if that is so, then, on the other hand, it is a Word that is also beyond all understanding: for its intrinsic transparency of meaning must remain opaquely mysterious to us because our bodies are opaque receivers of the mystery, are not yet themselves totally communicative, for our bodies, like formal speech, retain a surplus of unmeaning aural and visual materiality, sounds and shapes, over and above their capacities for meaning. And that is because, unlike Jesus's body, ours are not yet raised. It is because of his resurrection that Jesus's body is wholly present. But it is experienced in our bodies as absence because in our present historical contingency our bodies are not raised. Hence, what the Eucharist makes real is both the "now" of presence and the "not yet" of absence, the two intersecting and caught up into an eschatological, not a merely linear, temporality. Thomas's ontology, then, his account of the real, is essentially sacramental because it is essentially eschatological, inscribing in the body in its present condition an openness to a future that is not yet. The Eucharist is, then, an uncompleted eschatology realized as bodily exchange: the bread and wine become that body, a body which is all communication, the flesh made most perfectly to be Word, "Futurae gloriae nobis pignus datur," as Thomas says in one of his Eucharistic antiphons, wherein a "pledge is given to us of future glory."[33]

It is in all these respects that music both shows us what is central to reason and in doing so shows how reason is prototypically Eucharistic—at any rate we could mean that much by reason if we did not simply abase ourselves before the altar of that recent intellectual history which has reduced reason to that minimal sense of ratiocination. If music is a kind of spontaneous natural theology, it is because it is a kind of spontaneous natural eschatology. Which is, I think, why music, whether in mood it is happy or sad, is in a certain way that is characteristic of it as music, always sad. Music is the *lachrymae rerum*, the world's tears, its recollection now of what cannot yet be, past, present, and future, all in a chord or a cadence. At any rate, whether it is that weird and terrible trio of the Schubert string quintet, or the hushed moment of reconciliation of the finale of *The Mar-*

riage of Figaro—"Contessa perdono," sings the Count, "E dico di si," she replies—whichever it is at one end or the other of the emotional spectrum, or wherever between, all music makes you cry.[34] And I think it does so because music is in a way a shadow cast onto human sensibility of that eschatological temporality of the Eucharist. The sadness of music is a sort of sensual nostalgia for what one has caught some glimpse of but cannot yet possess, it is as it were, a premonition of a premonition; it is a shadow of the Augustinian *anamnesis,* a depth dug into memory,[35] scoring it with a sort of hope made real, but as loss and as absence, made present, but as yet to be real, it is our homeland glimpsed, but from a distance; the sadness of music is negative theology as inscribed in the body, in its tears.

THE EUCHARIST AND REASON

But if that is what is meant by reason in its maximal sense—that is, if it is our animal being insofar as it is the quasi-sacramental bearer of our self-transcendence, and if it is even among the primary ways leading out of a prematurely locked-in and instrumentalized notion of reason—then we take our final step to the conclusion, namely that that too is the shape which must be possessed by that very particular exercise of reason which I have been trying so hard till now to resist the reduction of reason to, that minimal sense which consists in ratiocination, in inference, in argument, and in proof.[36] Reason, for Thomas, is always bound to end up with God, so why not also that minimal form of it which is ratiocination? For reason in that sense of reasoning gives names to things, it names all of what music, through its very indeterminacy, its refusal of any constative character, can gesture toward but does not and cannot name, because naming is precisely what music doesn't do. But if reason, in this form as reasoning, names—it has to, naming is just what it does, being how the constative gets into human discourse at all—it does so also in the shadow of music's inarticulateness and indeterminacy, in the shadow of its apophatic refusal. For if reason can ever name God, it may do so only as that which finally defeats its powers: naming God is reason's supreme achievement but only insofar as in doing so it knows that what it so names escapes from under the naming, dodging all the arrows of naming that reason can fire at it. And it is that alone, as Thomas says, *quod omnes dicunt Deum*, naming so stretched out to the end of its tether that its tether finally snaps. In God reason reaches the point of collapse, because the theological over-loads it with significance. It is then, and only then, Thomas says, that it has got to the unknowable God. Only then can we with confidence agree on that "all": Christians, Muslims and Jews, but just as well those atheists it would be worthwhile having around to do their denying, engaging through their *oppositio* in an *eadem scientia*—at any rate we could if only atheists could be persuaded to engage in some decently radical level of denial that is not anyway surpassed by the theologians on their way to unknowing.

I have no intention of expounding, still less of defending in point of formal validity, those famous and much-derided five ways of Thomas Aquinas. I simply draw attention to the argument-strategy by which they work, for it has, as music has, the shape of the sacramental, the form of the body's transparency to the mystery we call "God." The same ontology is at work, the same negative theology in both. It is only through our bodies' in-timacy to the world's materiality that we achieve that glimpse of its ulti-mate significance that is the unknowable mystery of God. And herein is the paradox of our human rationality, of which, I say, music is the sign. When in *Prima pars*, question 2, article 3 of the *Summa theologiae* Thomas tells us that we can by those five ploys of inference prove the existence of God, he notes immediately afterwards in the prologue to question 3 that what proves God to exist also proves that as of God we have finally lost our grip on the meaning of *exist* itself, so that in proving God to exist we push rea-son by means of its own devices beyond its point of exhaustion. And so it is that by means of rational inference we do in a merely speculative way what the Eucharist draws us into the very life of. Reason gets you to where unnameable mystery begins but stands on this side of it, gesturing toward what it cannot know, and there it is self-emptied, "kenotically," as we might say; for it is stunned into a sort of babble at the shock of its final defeat—this reduction to babble, by the way, being what is otherwise called "the-ology." But by the Eucharist we are drawn into that same mystery as into our carnal life, so that we live by the mystery, we eat it, though the mystery is no more comprehensible, as Thomas says, for being eaten than it is for being thought. For he tells us that we do not resolve the mystery by faith as if it were some conundrum that reason could not solve yet to which faith on the other hand held the solution. For "we do not know what God is even by the revelation of grace": by grace, he says, we are indeed truly "made one with God" so as to share in the divine life, but "as to one who is unknown to us," *quasi ei ignoto coniungamur*.[37]

That, I think, is how we animals know God, whether by reason or by faith, at any rate according to Thomas. Put at its simplest, his position is formally that there are grounds of faith for affirming reason's autonomy, such that it can of its own resources know God by way of its characteristic exercise of argument. Reading Thomas alerts us not to confuse his baby of reason with the bathwater of rationalism. If unalerted you do confuse them, all sorts of unnecessary and theologically damaging zero-sum problems get called up to catch you out, trading off faith and reason against one another—at any rate, that is what Thomas seems to say. And so do I.

PART II

MYSTERY AND MYSTICISM

FOUR

Metaphor, Poetry, and Allegory

*Erotic Love in Bernard of Clairvaux
and John of the Cross*

FOUR THEOLOGIANS ON THE SONG OF SONGS

Though in the one thousand years of medieval commentary on the Song of Songs—from Gregory the Great in the sixth century to John of the Cross in the late sixteenth—its commentators seem often to suppose that they are working within a common and uniform tradition of scriptural interpretation, the constructions of the four senses of scripture to which they all appeal are in practice notoriously diverse, and frequently inconsistently employed. It is no use attempting to capture medieval exegetical theory or practice within a single clearly defined account of how those senses are to be distinguished, and if we do, if, for example, we take the theoretical exactness with which Thomas Aquinas distinguishes them as our starting point for the taxonomy of styles of the Song's medieval interpretation, we may indeed gain a certain clarity of perspective for the nonce, this being what constitutes the main temptation to start there. On the other hand, while it would clarify some things, others, I believe, would be thereby obscured, among them an important feature of Bernard of Clairvaux's readings of the Song in his eighty-six sermons.

In this chapter I will outline the shape and general form of a number of linked hypotheses. First, I posit that exegetical strategies in the Middle Ages vary across a spectrum far wider than they do today, and that they vary principally according to purpose. Second, I have a go at determining something about what Bernard of Clairvaux is doing in those sermons, and at setting that purpose in two relations of contrast: with the purpose which governs the exegetical strategies of Thomas Aquinas and others of his hermeneutical ilk, and then with what John of the Cross is doing in his poem the *Spiritual Canticle* and his prose gloss upon it. In this latter case, it is my further hypothesis that John's prose commentary is intended to stand in the same exegetical relation to his own poetic re-creation of the Song of Songs as he believes any exegesis should stand to the scriptural text itself. This, in turn, will suggest a more general speculation, provoked also by that most striking of impressions gained by anyone in the least acquainted with the standard medieval monastic Song commentary: namely, of the enormous gulf between the intense poetic eroticism of the Song itself and the generally bloodless pedantry of the commentarial tradition. The speculation is that it is a general purpose of much medieval monastic exegetical practice to evacuate the Song of its carnally erotic potential; that this is a purpose shared by John of the Cross, who in this respect at least is better understood as a late medieval ascetical exegete than as a protoromantic poet of the erotic; finally, that it is Bernard of Clairvaux above all others in whose eighty-six sermons is found some genuine feeling for and some commentarial participation in the eroticism of the Song's discourse.

THOMAS AQUINAS ON THE FOUR SENSES OF SCRIPTURE

Let us begin with some comments on Thomas Aquinas's distinctions between four senses of scripture as he formulates them in his *Quodlibet* 7, question 6.[1] The first comment may not seem particularly relevant, though it is in fact. It is that, if James Weisheipl is right, this text is not a *Quodlibet* at all, but a *Quaestio disputata*:[2] that is, it is not Thomas's response to his audience's agenda but a question he personally selected for debate, presumably because he attached some importance to it within his own priorities. And what importance Thomas may have attached to this particular disputation would become transparent if it were true, as again Weisheipl believes it to be, that Quodlibet 7, article 6, was one of four questions chosen for debate by Thomas in fulfillment of a very public and official duty: the requirement to dispute before the assembled Masters at Paris at his own inception as Master in 1256.[3]

If that last is true, then it should provide a clue as to Thomas's purpose in choosing to dispute this issue of the four senses, and perhaps as well some explanation of why he draws the distinctions between them in the way he does. For as a question disputed before fellow masters at his inception, we could expect it to have some character of a manifesto, a statement of his own program as theological master in his own right at a great theological school. It is not too hazardous to guess, therefore, that his decision to debate the senses of scripture on this occasion was meant to signal the importance Thomas attached to scripture as the foundation of the whole enterprise of school theology, a supposition whose plausibility is reinforced by his having situated the parallel discussion in the *Summa theologiae* within its very first question, on the nature and purpose of *sacra doctrina*, or "holy teaching," itself.[4] In short, what we may guess from this evidence is that the standpoint from which Thomas addresses the distinction of senses in two of the principal texts in which he explicitly discusses it is that, very particularly, of the Schoolman of theology at the University of Paris.

If that is a fair supposition, it is probably no more hazardous to guess that this program of defining the role of scripture within the theological methodology of the schools influenced not only Thomas's choice of subject for disputation at his inception but also the manner of his making the distinctions themselves. As a Parisian Master, Thomas was inevitably preoccupied with, among other things, the nature of theology as argument,[5] and therefore with the grounds on which sound argument in theology may be based, above all, of course, from scripture. And this in turn raised the question of which senses of scripture could serve as a firm enough grounding for a sound theological structure. That this was in fact Thomas's main concern is borne out by the manifest emphasis of both discussions, for in

both texts the case is the same: if the development of holy teaching involves argument, and if the foundations of it lie in scripture, then scripture must contain a sense that is without ambiguity, or else the whole
theological project is too vulnerable to fallacy, specifically the fallacy of
equivocation.[6] But, he goes on, any one passage of scripture is capable of
multiple readings of spiritual sense. For spiritual senses are based on likenesses (*similitudines imaginariae*) between one thing and another,[7] and
any two things can be like one another in any number of different ways,
and more or less at will. Therefore, theological argument can be based legitimately only on an unambiguously determinable literal sense, and in
both texts Thomas invokes Augustine's authority to emphasize the point:
"No argument about doctrine may be based on any but the literal sense,
as Augustine says in his letter to Vincentius the Donatist."[8]

I suspect a polemical point here. If in general terms programmatic
and declarative of the Schoolman's theological method, these discussions
are above all meant to exclude the arbitrary use of scripture in theological
argument, to which habits of neglect of the literal sense, common in the
standard monastic commentary, and leading to an excessive reliance on the
spiritual senses, left theologians all too vulnerable. And when we come to
the detail, in particular of his distinction between the literal and the three
spiritual senses, we can observe this concern motivating him again. Two aspects of his discussions show this rather more clearly than others. The first
is his insistence that *similitudines imaginariae* are part of the literal sense,[9]
and the second is that the literal sense of scripture is to be found in the
things and events (*res*) it refers to, things and events that must be historically true if the spiritual senses are to be legitimately founded upon them.[10]

As to the first, Thomas is determined to be clear about an issue on
which he evidently regarded many to be confused. The word *literal* as used
of a sense of scripture does not contrast, as it does in our own usage today,
with "metaphorical," for a metaphor is just another, albeit indirect, way of
referring with truth or falsity to some fact or event in the world. Poetry, he
thinks, is entirely written in metaphors,[11] and if we supposed that metaphors are nonliteral forms of speech and always yield a spiritual sense,
then we would have to suppose that all poetry is on a par with scripture in
yielding spiritual senses, which, of course, it is not. That being the case in
principle, Thomas concludes that even where in scripture the text is writ-

ten in metaphors, it is not by virtue of its metaphorical character as such that it possesses a spiritual sense, if, indeed, it possesses a spiritual sense at all. For any old human author can write in metaphors and make poems; but only the Holy Spirit can dispose scripture to yield up a spiritual sense.

What, then, determines the literal sense as distinct from the spiritual senses? Here again Thomas seeks clarity where he seems to think others are confused. And I paraphrase his argument in our terms rather than his, though I hope still accurately: the literal sense and only the literal sense is the meaning of the words of the text of scripture. Hence, whatever devices of speech are used, whatever trope contributes to the meaning of the text, these contribute to nothing but its literal sense. As we might put it, so far as the semantics of scripture are concerned, they are wholly exhausted by the literal sense. Or as Thomas himself puts it, "All that is part of the literal sense which can genuinely be got from the meaning of the words."[12] But, he goes on, it is not only words that are capable of signifying meanings, for the things (*res*) which are signified by the words of human authors are themselves capable, through the action of the Holy Spirit, of signifying too. Now if the literal sense is that which is signified by the words, then the spiritual senses are those further senses that are signified by the things the words signify. As he says: "The author of [all] things not only can make use of words to signify something but also can arrange for things to be figures of other things. Because of this the truth is made plain in sacred scripture in two ways. In one way insofar as things are signified by the words: and this is the literal sense. In another way by virtue of the fact that things are figures of other things: and this is what the spiritual sense consists in."[13]

Now it seems to follow from this that for Thomas the spiritual senses of scripture are not senses of the text itself—for only the literal sense is that. Rather, they are found in the signifying power of the historical events that scripture, in its literal sense, truly records. Anything at all that belongs to the text of the book is literal, whereas allegory, tropology, and anagogy are senses authored by the Holy Spirit in the text of providential history. From this follows the mistake of those who, confused about this distinction, derive opportunity for freelance and arbitrary allegorizing from the mere presence of metaphor in the language of scripture, who find in every utterance of poetry in scripture an alibi for a plurality of meanings such as would threaten theological discourse with equivocity. In short, for Thomas, poetry as such has no exegetical or spiritual significance; on the other hand scriptural poetry has great exegetical significance precisely insofar as it contributes to the literal sense of scripture, as, in the case of the Song of Songs, and of many another biblical text, the Psalms especially, it does.

NICHOLAS OF LYRA AND
THE LITERAL SENSE OF SCRIPTURE

Equally hostile to a common monastic partiality for free-range allegorizing, equally committed to the priority of the literal sense, but motivated by different exegetical purposes, is another friar, the Franciscan Master of the fourteenth century at Paris, Nicholas of Lyra. Broadly, at any rate in the methodological introduction to his *Postilla litteralis* on scripture, his distinction of senses follows Thomas.[14] But for Nicholas the Song of Songs presents a particular problem not raised for his theoretical literalism by other texts of the Old Testament. To all appearances the Song is a collection of bawdy poems about a corrupt sexual liaison between unmarried partners. But a text consisting in so unworthy a narrative cannot be what the Holy Spirit calls for spiritual meanings to be founded in. Hence, the literal referent of the Song cannot consist in the adulterous love affair between Solomon and the Shulamite woman.[15] But if not in that narrative, in what can the literal sense consist?

Nicholas's answer is ingenious and generates a way of reading of the Song very nearly unique in the Western medieval period. It is to treat its entire first six chapters as an extended series of metaphors (*parabola*) not for Christological mysteries but for the history of Israel, with that history in turn serving, as on Thomas's account it should, as the foundation in historical fact (*res*) for allegory. Now this solution also depends upon a clear decision to follow Thomas and to treat all metaphor as part of the literal sense, since it is by metaphor that the Song literally denotes the Jewish history which, in turn, forms the basis of allegory. In turn, this move restores to prominence, from its condition of suppression in standard monastic-allegorical exegesis, the foundation of Christian interpretation of the Hebrew scriptures in their Jewish truth: the *sensus litteralis* becomes again, as it did once before in the twelfth century for Andrew of St. Victor, the *sensus hebraicus*.

It does so all the more visibly in the anonymous *Expositio hystorica* on the Song composed sometime in the late thirteenth century[16]—although Nicholas appears not to know of it. This *Expositio* is written *secundum Salomonem*, that is to say, following the hermeneutical principles of Rabbi Solomon ben Isaac, or "Rashi," the Jewish commentator of the eleventh century in Paris. Composed by a Christian scholar, the *Expositio hystorica* is a Latin adaptation and paraphrase of Rashi's commentary, designed to follow Rashi as closely as possible, that is, as far as is consistent with an orthodox Christian interpretation.

There is no need to dwell on the revisions of Rashi's interpretation necessary to draw it into consistency with orthodox Christian belief,[17] for what matters is that in principle, of course, any Christian attempt to read the Song in Rashi's terms is bound to focus upon the common ground in a literal sense. For there, as in Nicholas, the anonymous Latinizing Christian can readily identify the literal sense with the *sensus hebraicus*. Consequently, following Rashi along a path of theoretical hermeneutics laid down already by Thomas and later to be followed by Nicholas, our Christian author composes an interpretation of the Song that is both in the strict sense literal and at the same time not, in this literal sense, to be understood as the narrative of the mutual love of Solomon and the Shulamite woman. The author manifestly regards his position as consistent: the Song is both literally about and metaphor for the history of Israel. He says:

Solomon . . . composed this work in [the guise of] a metaphor of a woman who was made a widow by her husband's desertion while he was still alive, and she desires and longs to be restored to him and to be united to him by love, remembering as she does the love of her youth. The Bridegroom himself suffers for her in her misery, remembering the kindnesses of her youth and her beauty and honest behavior, which united her with him by powerful bonds of love; and he does so on this account, that he has not willingly afflicted her, nor has he rejected her unconditionally, for she is still his wife and he her husband.[18]

As the editors of the Latin text argue, this reading of the Song as pure metaphor is consistent with its author's claim to be offering an *expositio hystorica* only on that principle first clearly argued for by Hugh of St. Victor in the twelfth century and by Thomas more systematically in the thirteenth, namely that metaphor is part of the literal sense.[19] To which one can add that though Nicholas does not know the Latin *Expositio*, he certainly does know his Rashi. And all three agree on the following three hermeneutical propositions as regards the interpretation of the Song: first, that it is not literally about the love of Solomon and the Shulamite woman; second, that it is a work composed entirely of metaphor; and third, that the literal sense carried by the Song's metaphors is found in their reference to the history of Israel's relationship with her God.

The significance of this to our purposes is to remove support for a widespread and mistaken assumption. That assumption is that as medieval commentaries on the Song go, better justice is done to the authenticity of the Song's erotic text and texture the more attention is paid to its literal sense, and that the remorselessly allegorizing and spiritualizing techniques of the monastic tradition—of Gregory, Bede and the *Glossa ordinaria*, Alcuin, Honorius of Autun, Rupert of Deutz, Alain de Lille, or Thomas Gallus—are alone responsible for the erotic pallidness of the medieval commentarial tradition. Not so. In point of erotic pallidness scarcely anything in the whole Middle Ages matches the reduction in sexual tension of Nicholas of Lyra's terse but pedantic historicism; scarcely any medieval commentary provides so stark a contrast as does his between the rich, full-blooded eroticism of the text itself and the commentary upon it.

BERNARD OF CLAIRVAUX AND
DENYS THE CARTHUSIAN ON THE SONG

Nonetheless, on the score of theoretical precision of hermeneutic, Thomas, and Nicholas following him, are at least clear. But, I suggest, theirs is a dangerous and misleading clarity if one reads other traditions of medieval scriptural commentary quite generally and often unfavorably in the light of those distinctions so precisely made. Above all, on the presuppositions of Scholastic exegesis we can be tempted to ask of Bernard of Clairvaux just how clear he is about these things in his *Sermons on the Song of Songs*. And the answer to that question, addressed in any such terms to Bernard, can only be that Bernard is thoroughly confused as to hermeneutical theory and method.

Just how confused Bernard can look if you read his exegetical practice in the light of a Thomas Aquinas or a Nicholas of Lyra is easily illustrated by the following passage from *Sermon* 9.7:

> While the Bride is conversing about the Bridegroom, he, . . . , suddenly appears, yields to her desire by giving her a kiss. . . . The swelling of her breasts is proof of this. For so great is the potency of that holy kiss, that no sooner has the bride received it than she conceives and her breasts grow rounded with the fruitfulness of conception, bearing witness, as it were, with this milky abundance. Men with an urge to frequent prayer will have experience of what I say. Often enough when we approach the altar our hearts are dry and lukewarm. But if we persevere, there comes an unexpected infusion of grace, our breast expands, as it were and our interior is filled with an overflowing love; and if someone were to press upon it then, this milk of sweet fecundity would gush forth in streaming richness. Let us hear the bridegroom: "You have received, my love, what you asked for, and here is a sign to show you, your breasts are better than wine; henceforth you will know that you have received the kiss because you will be conscious of having conceived. That explains the expansion of your breasts, filled with a milky richness far surpassing the wine of worldly knowledge that can intoxicate indeed but with curiosity, not charity; it fills but does not nourish; puffs up but does not build up; pampers but does not strengthen."[20]

Evidently you could ask of this passage, which is it, metaphor or allegory? In a more huffily pedantic spirit still, you could ask whether Bernard does not mistakenly suppose that he is giving a properly allegorical reading of the Bride's breasts when in fact all he is doing is extruding theological and spiritual lessons out of a rather overworked, and really rather tasteless, metaphor. For after all, the connection between the swelling of a pregnant woman's breasts and the expanding bosom of meditative prayer is established only through what Thomas was later to call *similitudines imaginariae*, not as he and Nicholas thought was required by properly founded allegory, through the Holy Spirit's providential determination of real historical connections between Solomon's love for the Shulamite woman and the redemptive purposes of God. The "likenesses" Bernard establishes between the language of the Song and the tropological discourse of his interpretation are abstract, dehistoricized, and, one has to say, often far-fetched exploitations of metaphors, where they are not mere similes. In that spirit you could say Bernard is just confused about that concerning which Thomas and Nicholas are determined to be clear, namely, that whereas metaphor is, allegory is not, part of the meaning of the text and that if you want a properly founded theology you had better beware of extracting theological conclusions from fanciful allegories. Well, you could say this, indeed inevitably you would, were you to insist upon pressing the exigencies of an appropriately Scholastic method of interpretation upon Bernard.

But I think it would be wrong to do this, and wrong for a reason that goes well beyond the obvious anachronism of forcing a twelfth-century Cistercian's Song exegesis into the mold of a thirteenth-century Schoolman of Paris. The reason, I guess, is more general and has to do with fundamental differences of exegetical purpose. First, Thomas's distinctions belong within a conscious methodological project dictated by the needs of a biblical hermeneutic appropriate for a systematic theology in the mode of the schools. There, those distinctions are needed, and they need to be made with the precision with which Thomas and Nicholas make them. Bernard's reading of the Song, however, is made within a quite different, because homiletic, purpose, where the principal concern is not with epistemologically secure foundations for a dialectical theology but with the practical direction of Cistercian monks. Bernard's concern is therefore not with the literal meanings on which a theological edifice can be built but with the impact of his speech on lives; he is therefore less concerned with what the words of the Song in some formal academically theological sense of the word *literal* literally say than with what his saying them does; not, then, with literal truth-bearing properties of language but with the character of utterance as speech act; not with exegetical truth, but with a homiletic and pastoral rhetoric. "Hodie . . ." he says as if to emphasize to his Cistercian brethren his homiletic purposes ". . . legimus in libro experientiae" (Today we read in the book of *experience*).[21]

For this reason Bernard's reading of the Song is more preoccupied with the erotic quality of the language itself, which he clearly values more in its capacity for spiritual arousal than in any narrative truth it may possess, a matter on which he is largely silent. At the outset he declares that his fascination with the Song is for its language, not for its literal truth: he values it precisely because it is a "figurative language" and as such "pregnant with delight,"[22] thereby eroticizing nicely his metaphor for its eroticism. The Song's language is a "melody . . . the very music of the heart . . . an inward pulsing of delight . . . [that] only the singer hears . . . and the one to whom he sings—the lover and the beloved,"[23] and in more general terms he praises the quality of this language for its spiritual appropriateness: "No sweeter names can be found to embody that sweet interflow of affections between the Word and the soul, than bridegroom and bride. Between these all things are equally shared, there are no selfish reservations, nothing that causes division. They share the same inheritance, the same table, the same marriage-bed, they are flesh of each other's flesh."[24] And again he says of the Song's opening words, "Let him kiss me with the kiss of his mouth": "How delightful a ploy of speech [is] this, prompted into life by the kiss, with Scripture's own engaging countenance inspiring the reader and enticing him on, that he might find pleasure even in the laborious pursuit of what lies hidden, with a fascinating theme to sweeten the fatigue of research. Surely this mode of beginning that is not a beginning, this novelty of diction in a book so old, cannot but increase the reader's intention."[25]

Bernard could hardly be more positive in his welcome to that feature of the Song's language and imagery which, for many another monk, was the chief stimulus to burrow beneath it for alternative, more "spiritual" meanings: the Song's explicit, baroque eroticism. Erotic frankness appears not to worry Bernard at all. On the contrary, he revels in it. But it did worry most monks. And it worried the friar Nicholas of Lyra. That is why if Thomas had reasons of systematic theology for carefully distinguishing the four senses, the average monk, sharing little of Thomas's Scholastic interests, had an equally powerful, if very different, reason for distinguishing them: for the average monastic commentator the literal eroticism of the Song's language threatened carnal danger both personal and exegetical, and the interpretative schema of the four senses provided an exegetical method for the spiritualization of its carnality. Wholly in contrast with the rhetorical confidence of Bernard of Clairvaux is the exegetical timidity of the fifteenth-century Flemish Carthusian Denys van Rykel, who is much troubled by the temptations that will afflict the minds of the spiritually immature when reading this text, which "on the surface seems so very sensual but on a true understanding proves to be very spiritual."[26] For, he asks, "[What] is to be done for those many religious and canons and others in holy orders who in church and in the divine office will commonly hear or read these words, though they are not yet purified, who have hardly attained to a true and spiritual understanding and can scarcely read and hear these words at those times . . . without lewd imaginings? I think that they are to be advised to strive as far as possible to understand this book with purity of mind and in its true sense"—which for Denys, of course, is anything but the literal—if they are to "leave behind them every kind of unbecoming thought."[27]

Connected with this pious scruple there is in Denys, as there is not in Bernard, a very characteristic medieval monastic inversion. Few would have verbally contradicted Bernard's praise for the eroticism of the Song's language as image, intensely worrying as it was to many and lacking, as most were, in his outright enthusiasm for it. At all costs, however, the poem's carnality has to be denied any literal value, and, as Denys insists, "They are mistaken who think that this work should be read in its literal and historical sense as referring to Solomon and his bride, the daughter of Pharaoh [he says he has in mind Nicholas of Lyra] and [only] allegorically to Christ and the church. If this were so then the subject matter of this book would be of no worth, sensual and prurient and not spiritual, mystical, most excellent and heavenly; nor would it be a prophetic text, but rather a sort of love song."[28]

For which reason, insofar as Denys attaches any value to the erotic carnality of the Song's language it is as pure, but abstract, image, and the meaning that image evokes is purely spiritual, realized most typically in the monastic way of life itself. Hence arises the need for a radical inversion of the Song's language and imagery. For Denys the Carthusian it is the monk who truly effects by his celibacy what the Song's eroticism images by way of its carnality. Carnal marriage between woman and man is the sign, but the monk's mystical marriage to Christ is the reality signified. By means of allegory the carnal sign is successfully emptied into its spiritual significance. By this style of allegory the text is denied its biblical significance as poetry.

But this exegetical inversion is not there in Bernard, because he does not need it. Bernard appears less threatened by the Song's carnality of image, and for that reason his sermons differ very markedly in rhetorical tone not only from classical monastic commentaries of his own times and later but also from the standard Scholastic commentary of the next century and beyond—as I have indicated, Nicholas of Lyra's literal *Postilla* is every bit as bloodless a thing rhetorically as is Denys's hyperbolical allegorizing. Bernard's discourse resists that de-eroticization of the Song's carnality: on the contrary, he enthusiastically places that carnality in the foreground, emphasizing its erotic density. Bernard foregrounds the carnal image, and for that reason the spiritually sensual reading so characteristic of Bernard's *Sermons* quite defies analysis in terms of the hermeneutical schema of the four senses and is, in my view, obscured by the attempt to impose it. In short, though clearly Bernard knows and assumes standard twelfth-century categorizations of literal and spiritual senses and sometimes consciously uses them, his employment of the erotic discourse of the Song is principally in the interests of a homiletic rhetoric of speech act, not in those of a scientific exegesis of meaning, and in the eroticization of the spiritual, not in spiritualization of the carnal. Hence his *Sermons* ought to be read not principally as allegory but principally as poetry. In consequence, the doctrine of the four senses, as it came to him in the monastic traditions he inherited mainly, if somewhat distantly, from Origen and Gregory the Great, could not have served any but the contrary of his poetic purpose, which was, if anything, best served by the rhetorical heightening of the Song's erotic tensions, not their exegetical slackening, and by a rhetorical thickening of the erotic textures, not by their spiritualized evacuation. Bernard, in my view, is a poet matching the Song's poetry with a poetic reading of his own. Perhaps surprisingly, one could not say the same of John of the Cross, for all that his first hermeneutical act in respect of the Song is to rewrite it as his own poem.

JOHN OF THE CROSS AND THE SONG

For when we turn to our sixteenth-century Spanish poet, we are brought back to the difficult question of the relationship between the poem and the prose commentary of the *Spiritual Canticle*. And let me begin with the (of course) contestable proposition that John's prose commentary may legitimately be seen to stand to his poem in much the same relationship as the traditional monastic commentary stands to the Song of Songs. In the teeth of modern Sanjuanist scholarship, I believe that this can be a helpful way to look at the matter, even if there is one important and obvious respect in which this comparison fails. The medieval commentator on the Song was not the author of the text he construed; he was only the author of his own commentary on it. The commentator knew that the principal author of the Song was the Holy Spirit. He knew,[29] particularly if he was of an allegorizing inclination in the manner of Denys the Carthusian, that the text he was presented with was only a surface and that though the Holy Spirit had shaped that surface too, he had done so only to disguise or hide beneath it the deeper, spiritual meanings which, in turn, are the determinants of the contours of the surface. The medieval commentator therefore saw himself as faced with a quasi-geological problem of reading the mind of the Creator who had buried unknown meanings in unknown places below the surface. Moreover, when he faced the problem of how to identify the lower geological strata, he was possessed of but one instrument of measurement and one set of clues as to where to apply it.

The clues were the cracks and fissures on the surface, the anomalous ruptures in the literal meaning—the numerous factual inconsistencies, the hyperbole, the absurd comparisons, and the outrageous metaphors with which scripture is intentionally littered—intentionally, it was said,[30] so that the reader's mind would be distracted from the literal meaning, enticed into its spiritual. The measuring instrument was the power of allegory. Applied to the surface anomaly, the allegorical method was capable of reading off networks of correspondence between surface and depth with which the commentator could ultimately map the whole of the surface on to its sustaining substructure. Thereafter, if the commentator chose, he could mine those depths too and appropriate the gold of the spiritual meanings to himself in a moral—or, as he called it, a "tropological"—interpretation.

Nonetheless, though John owes much to this tradition, his commentary cannot stand to his poem in exactly the same relationship as the biblical commentator's to the Song, for the simple reason that John, unlike the biblical commentator, was the author of both. In other respects, however, the comparison holds. For John, the author of his commentary is the interpreter of the poem's spiritual meanings. But he is also the author of the poem that, as interpreter, he expounds. It is therefore John who disguises as poet what John the interpreter reveals. In short, John is to the conjunction of poem and prose what the Holy Spirit is, on the traditional medieval account, in relation to the double meaning of the Song, the author at once of surface and depth, and of the relation between them.

This is not the fanciful suggestion that it might seem to be. We have John's own words for it that, in the description of the relationship between commentary and poem, the analogy is his too. Though he pretends to stand back from his authorial relationship with the poem so as to speak of himself in the role of commentator, as if of another's work, nothing can disguise from us, still less from John of the Cross, the fact that he is the author too of that which he proposes to interpret:

> If [the] similitudes [of his *Spiritual Canticle*] are not read with the simplicity of the spirit of knowledge and love which they contain, they will seem to be absurdities rather than reasonable utterances, as will those comparisons of the divine Canticle of Solomon and other books of Sacred Scripture where the Holy Spirit, unable to express the fullness of His meaning in ordinary words, utters mysteries in strange figures and likenesses. The saintly doctors, no matter how much they have said or will say, can never furnish an exhaustive explanation of these figures and comparisons, since the abundant meanings of the Holy Spirit cannot be caught in words. Thus the explanation of these expressions usually contains less than what they in themselves embody.[31]

This, as a model for interpretation, is already in his time ancient, stretching back across fourteen centuries of elaboration and development in monastic exegesis in the West, to Origen in the East. Here is how Origen himself puts it:

> [The Holy Spirit's] aim is to envelop and hide secret mysteries in or dinary words under the pretext of a narrative of some kind and an account of visible things. . . . Moreover, we should know that since the

chief aim of the Holy Spirit was to keep the logical order of the spiritual meaning either in what is bound to happen or in what has already taken place, if anywhere he found that what had happened according to the narrative could be fitted to the spiritual meaning, He composed something woven out of both kinds in a single verbal account, always hiding the secret meaning more deeply. But where the narrative of events could not be coherent with the spiritual logic, He sometimes interspersed either events less likely or absolutely impossible to have happened and sometimes events that could have happened but in fact did not.[32]

That, precisely, is the relationship in which John stands to his *Canticle*, the poem itself to the prose commentary.

But because he stands to them both as the Holy Spirit stands to the Song, John knows the spiritual meaning of his poem in advance. He writes the poetic surface so as at once to disguise and reveal the depth, for he creates both the surface contours and the depths that sustain them. His poem will seem to contain "absurdities" and "strange figures and likenesses" (the fractured narrative, the kaleidoscopic imagery) because he himself wrote them into it, already knowing what spiritual meanings explain them. In that same sense in which, for Origen, the hidden spiritual meaning generates or "writes" the surface, literal meaning of the scriptural text, so too, in John's literary output; hence the natural relationship—at any rate as we postromantic literary critics would see it—between poem and prose is reversed. In an important authorial sense the prose was already there as spiritual meaning before the poem came to exist as carnal image. And so it can be for the reader too, who may *prefer* the poems to the prose, who may read John's intent in the poem and leave the prose alone. But what cannot be denied is that the meaning of the *Spiritual Canticle* is prosaic, because it is already given in the traditions of spiritual interpretation of the Song of Songs: you can get the gist of John's mystical theology from the poems only because of those traditions.

It is plain, however, that this is not how contemporary Sanjuanist scholars prefer to see the matter. Overwhelmingly, the weight of recent critical opinion, Spanish and anglophone, is on the side of the case for the priority of the poetry over the prose, for the singularity of the poem over and against the generality of its commentary. Barnstone, for example, confidently affirms that "while the commentaries depend on the poems, the poems do not depend on the commentaries, and are often distorted by them; it is not necessary to know the commentaries in order to understand the poems."[33] He dismisses as "literary heresy" and as the "intentional fallacy" the procedure of reading the poetry in terms of the significance that John finds for them in the prose commentaries.[34] More generally, the received opinion favors the standing of the literary, emotional, and spiritual qualities of the poetry as they can be understood in their own right, so it is fashionable to emphasize the poetry's own intensity of passion, the sensuality of the imagery in its own terms, the authenticity of the poet's love of nature for its own sake, and, in respect of literary sources and models, the dependence not so much on the prose theological commentaries as on secular precedents, in particular on the popular love songs and dance forms of his native Spain.[35]

What I have had to say about the relationship between the poetry and the prose of John of the Cross implies the opposite of all this. I think it plain that the commentaries could very easily be made to stand on their own as independent treatises—indeed, for good or ill, for several centuries they were so read and still frequently are, and as making perfectly good, complete, sense on their own terms. And as far as the poetry is concerned, the existence of the commentaries from John's own hand has the result that the poetry cannot now stand on its own. Perhaps we could say that if the commentaries had not been written, the poems could have stood on their own, though even then they would do so because of their reliance for their meaning upon the patristic and medieval traditions of Song exegesis. That said, the commentaries have been written by John's own hand, and as a result it cannot be a mistake to take poetry and prose in conjunction. In any case, for the Carmelite sisters of the convent at Beas at least, who because they, like all women of their times, were not permitted to read the full text of the biblical poems and so requested of John that he write the commentary, so opaque did they find the poetry, the poems patently did not stand on their own. Moreover, the point is not merely logical: in the case of the *Spiritual Canticle*, the poem is designed to be so fractured in narrative sequence and in overall significance as to demand a gloss—and not merely because of the reader's ignorance of the significance but because the text is specifically designed to point beyond itself to the sorts of meaning ascribed to it by the commentaries.

None of this is to deny that the poetry and the prose are different genres, nor is it to suppress the importance of their differing literary qualities. Neither could displace the other without some loss of what each uniquely provides. After all, John himself says as much. If he acknowledges, in the spirit of the biblical exegete, the need to answer the request of the nuns of Beas for an explanation, he is every bit as emphatic in denying that the prose explanations can exhaust every legitimate significance of the poems: they do not, he insists, supply the only possible meanings of the poems. Nor is any of this to deny that John wrote the poems without any thought for the prose commentaries upon them; and it is consistent to concede that in some ways the poems are the more fundamental and primary literary output within John's oeuvre. On the other hand, it is at least to raise a question about how to judge their character as poetry, and it is in this respect worth countering the modern prejudice that, if the poems were read as they stand in a premodern and distinctly preromantic relationship with the prose commentaries on them, they would just because of that cease to be fine poetry. There is no need to draw that conclusion from the obvious fact that John of the Cross is not Wordsworth.

A LATE MEDIEVAL HERMENEUTIC

Precisely because it is necessary to read John of the Cross on his own terms it is necessary not to read the poetry in isolation from his prose. This holds true at the hermeneutical level, where we are faced with the fact that the poetry and the prose come down to us from John's hand together with an explicitly stated set of principles for the interpretation of the relationship between them. That hermeneutic is a late medieval, not a modern, postromantic one. John shows no sign of valuing any literary product for its own sake and simply as literary. Nor does he show any sign of valuing poetry as a genre that is uniquely irreplaceable. His conviction that the poetry contains a surplus of significances beyond the reach of any commentary, including even his own, owes more to an Origenist scriptural hermeneutic than to any modern romantic doctrine of the uniqueness and self-sufficiency of the work of art. There is something anachronistic and un-historical in the contemporary insistence that John's poetry is devalued by being set in the relation he envisages for it with the prose commentaries.

Moreover, the setting of John's poetry against its medieval precedents is just as important in assessing the eroticism of the poem itself as in assessing the relationship of the prose to the poetry. And as to the poem itself, it may indeed be true that at least it is imitative of the styles and vocabularies of the Song's own love poetry. Yet no one can fail to be struck by how different is the Song's concrete immediacy and sexual explicitness from the distanced, abstract eroticism of John's *Canticle*. The monk has to interpret the Song spiritually, so vibrantly alive is it in erotic danger and risk. The *Canticle* runs no such risk today, nor ever did for a sixteenth-century reader: it is as safe as Psalms, for its spiritual meanings—and the fact that it has them—are perfectly transparent to any readers John himself could have envisaged, if only, unlike the sisters of Beas, they were equipped, as John could count on them being, with a knowledge of the traditions of Song interpretation on which the *Canticle* so manifestly depends. If the *Canticle* can stand on its own independently of the prose, this is because the reader already knows from centuries of exegetical tradition how to read it spiritually, and knows for each image and trope of the poem exactly how the tradition requires him to read it.

Indeed, the language of the *Canticle* betrays all too clearly the pressures to spiritualize that are exerted upon it. The eroticism of John's poem is two-dimensional and transparent, a sheet of glass superimposed upon its spiritual significances. Like a plate of glass it can shimmer and glitter, reflecting a light that strikes the eye, but only at one very precise, carefully contrived, angle of refraction. From any other angle that language is pure transparency, and, since it lacks any density of its own, lacks the erotic thickness of Bernard's rhetoric, we are compelled to look straight through it to what lies below. So it is with the erotic imagery of the *Canticle*. Again and again, as in stanza 31, we are given a brief moment of true erotic promise:

That one solitary hair
You looked upon it fluttering on my neck
You gazed at it on my neck
And it enchanted you. . . .

But immediately, the intrusive, calculated, Origenist absurdity of the next line, culled from the Song, pulls us back from the brink of carnal immediacy to the safety of the spiritual meaning:

And in one of my eyes I wounded you.[36]

The stilted, discordant image of a "single eye" may serve its Origenist purpose of reminding us that this stanza cannot be meant to evoke the carnally erotic stimulus of the woman's fluttering tresses, but rather to evoke the spiritual sense of the stanza. But it cannot be denied that it is, for those who seek an autonomous erotic significance, a disappointment. And, from the literary point of view—if you insist upon it—it is a contrived discordance, organized for an Origenist exegetical purpose: to ensure, by the allusion to the familiar sacred text whose spiritual meaning the reader already knows, that the metaphorical surface can be gotten to disappear into its spiritual interpretation.

For this reason it is possible, if only with some irony, to welcome the comment of the Spanish literary critic Menendez y Pelago: "So sublime is this poetry that it scarcely seems to belong to this world at all; it is hardly capable of being assessed by literary criteria."[37] Just so. The *Canticle* can hardly be assessed by "literary criteria" because it is not really literature at all, but good old-fashioned medieval Song hermeneutic. The effect created by the *Canticle* is indeed otherworldly and deliberately so. John the poet strives, it seems, to avoid the concrete image in its carnality and rather to create a smooth surface that is transparent to the deeper meaning below, to spiritualize the carnal lest the carnal displace the spiritual. The verse points beyond itself, urging the reader not to rest in it as poetry but to transcend it as spiritual theology.

———

To conclude. Nicholas of Lyra draws on Thomas to foreground the Song's literal meaning, but only to wrest from its metaphors all traces of the Song's carnality. John of the Cross writes in the Song's own poetic forms but has the prose mind of the medieval exegete, for his metaphors are more strictly allegories designed to be passed through on the way to their given spiritual meanings. Bernard writes in the prose forms of medieval allegory but has the truer poet's mind, for his allegories are rather the more genuine metaphors, their erotically charged textures flushing the spiritual with a carnal sensuality. There is no doubt in my mind which of these commentaries is closer in poetic texture to the carnal immediacy of the Song itself: in Bernard of Clairvaux the spiritual is disclosed by the carnal; in John of the Cross the carnal is displaced in the interests of the spiritual.

FIVE

Why Was Marguerite Porete Burned?

On June 1, 1310, Marguerite Porete, said to have been a "onetime Beguine" of Hainault, was burned at the stake in Paris as a relapsed heretic for having continued to allow the circulation of her work *The Mirror of Simple Souls*. Some years previously, at any rate prior to 1306, the work itself had been condemned for its heretical teachings by Guy II, bishop of Cambrai, and cast into the flames at Valenciennes,[1] and Marguerite forbidden to possess or promote it.

Even those bare facts are of very great historical significance. First, and in general terms, Marguerite's is the first known execution of a woman condemned for heretical teaching. And while of course we all know that women in the Middle Ages were generally thought not to be in possession of sufficiently acute mental powers to have significant theological opinions of any kind, on the evidence of her trial Marguerite was also thought to be sufficiently capable of well-formulated heresies that she could be required to recant them.

Second, particular issues are raised by the fact of a fourteenth-century woman being judged heretical, especially a Beguine in 1310, since at that time hostility to the Beguine and Beghard movements was rising to one of its episodic peaks of intensity, culminating, though by no means ceasing, in the condemnations of their teachings and practices as heretical at the Council of Vienne of 1311–12. But beyond these general and particular reasons three things about Marguerite's case mark it out for especial scrutiny, and it is with those that I shall be concerned in this chapter.

The first is that though she is thought with virtual certainty to have once been a Beguine, she could not have been the obvious Beguine to get at on the score of doctrine. For though there are some characteristically Beguine themes in her *Mirror* her spiritual teaching also departs in some very significant respects from what we know of Beguine teaching and practice—indeed, the *Mirror* can often look more like a critique of certain aspects of standard Beguine piety than an endorsement of them.[2] So doctrinally she was an atypical Beguine if at the time she was one at all, and she would not have served as a very central bull's-eye on a Beguine target. In this respect she bears some comparison with Meister Eckhart, who some sixteen years later was in trouble with the archbishop of Cologne, Henry of Virneberg; and if Oliver Davies is right this too was on account of his association with Beguines in Strasburg and Cologne, although, like Marguerite, he was willing to offer only critical support of their spiritual ways.[3] In any case, if hostility to Beguines motivated the harassment of Marguerite, she does seem an odd case to make an example of on the grounds of her teaching.

Second, as to that spiritual teaching itself, it was not so manifestly heterodox as all that, if at all. Later I will consider Marguerite's theology itself in connection with one doctrine of hers that seemed especially to trouble her inquisitors, concerning the role of the virtues in the life of "perfected" or "annihilated" souls. Here we may limit ourselves to the question of what reception the teachings of the *Mirror* might reasonably have had in her times—and how they were in fact received—by her contemporaries or near contemporaries. And immediately one wonders at the judgment of the *Mirror* as heretical, not, surprisingly, by the standards of our perceptions of orthodoxy today, but by the standards of her contemporaries. For if any medieval text could be expected to arouse suspicions in a post-Reformation Christian mind about the orthodoxy of medieval high mysticism, the heady dialectical Neoplatonism of the *Mirror* could be expected to do so, whereas, though a fourteenth-century ecclesiastical authority who really wanted to get at her work for some reason or other could easily find a theologian to construe its teaching as heterodox, he would have been bound to start an argument with other theologians happy to find a perfectly acceptable sense in it. If controversial, the *Mirror*'s teaching is recognizably the development of a tradition of apophatic, or negative, theology and spirituality that few in the fourteenth century could have dared call heretical as such.[4]

And both in her lifetime and subsequently, there were distinguished supporters of her teaching in respectable circles. Marguerite herself managed to persuade three theologians, John of Querayn, Frank Cantor, and Godfrey of Fontaines, to write more or less enthusiastic letters of endorsement, extracts from which she tacked on to the *Explicit* of her work, at some point probably after the Valenciennes condemnation of it.[5] More significantly, within decades of the condemnation of 1310 the work was circulating anonymously and quite widely, and apparently without causing more than the most occasional doubt or the mildest of qualifications. Lerner reports that there were three complete MSS in Latin translation from the fourteenth century and a fragment of a fourth; there are two independent Italian translations, also of the fourteenth century, and Lerner details evidence of thirty-six copies of the *Mirror* circulating in Italy in the fifteenth.[6] Scholars of late medieval English literature will be familiar with the fourteenth-century Middle English version that provides evidence of the extent of its circulation in Marguerite's Old French version, for the ME text appears to have been translated from the vernacular original, not, as one might have expected, from the Latin translation compiled for the purposes of the heresy trial. And then late in the fifteenth century the Carthusian Richard Methley retranslated the ME version back into Latin. If, as Lerner comments, this is not to say that there were no doubts about the book's orthodoxy, it is to say that they were not universally thought serious.[7] And, of course, much has been made by scholars of our own time of the fact that the work could circulate innocently when detached from its associations with the condemned heretic Marguerite and from hers with the Beguines, but not when her female authorship and her Beguine connection were known.[8] It is only natural to suppose that something not entirely free of vested interest was going on in the original condemnation and not just genuine doubts about the orthodoxy, in themselves, of her ideas. And since Marguerite's case is studied less by theologians than by

historians, who are professionally vulnerable to persuasion of under-
lying political motivation and less motivated to read a theological text
theologically, there has been too little study of Marguerite's teachings in
themselves and in relation to the continuing traditions in the fourteenth
century of apophatic (or "negative") theology.[9] This is a pity, for it is not
obvious that conspiracy alone will fully explain the complexity of Marguerite's case, a complexity that appears to derive at least from the inter-
penetration of factors of ecclesial interest combined with hostility to the
daring theological speculations of a lay woman, these reinforcing what are
more understandable and even perfectly sincere anxieties about the orthodoxy of her theology.

More of that later. In the meantime, prima facie these two things seem
odd about Marguerite's case: if heterodoxy was the target it seems strange
to select a text so readily capable of an orthodox interpretation; and if the
target was the Beguines by association it seems odd to pick on someone
whose ideas depart significantly from theirs. But there is a third oddity,
Marguerite's silence at her theological examination. She refused to take
the oaths necessary for the trial to proceed, and she further refused to answer any of the questions addressed to her by her Dominican prosecutor,
the inquisitor general of France, William Humbert. No doubt her silence
was a provocation, and presumably it was taken as in itself sufficient evidence of ill will, since the procedure required of her a formal recantation of
the heretical doctrines she was accused of maintaining, and by her policy
of silence she refused to give it. There can be little doubt also that she was
well aware of the risks she was taking. But we have no certain idea why she
refused to clarify her position. She could easily have done so. She could
easily have conceded, as later Eckhart did in his case to the inquisitorial
committee in Avignon, that the propositions extracted from the *Mirror*
and judged heretical were certainly dubious when taken out of context,
and then shown how in context they were carefully and subtly qualified
in ways quite capable of an orthodox, indeed traditional, interpretation.[10]
At any rate she could have tried, and the dialectical sophistication required to succeed in principle was far from exceeding her powers. But she
did not, and of speculations as to why, McGinn's is the most plausible.
Hers, he says, is a book about how to disappear, not just in its being about
annihilation of self, but even more primordially in being a book that self-

annihilates: to have defended it *in propria persona* would have been to affirm the authorial self in a text the point of which was to effect her disappearance.[11]

Thus a good reason why Marguerite's case might be of interest to the student of medieval apophaticism is that she was the first mystical theologian of the late Middle Ages to have faced formal charges of heresy for having proposed a strong, indeed radical, negative anthropology, an account of human selfhood and its negation corresponding with a more traditional negativity about the knowledge of God. Above all she was in trouble on account of her teaching that, for the perfected soul in the nothingness of God, she is God's nothingness, she is "one" with it.[12] For this reason the place of her teachings within the developing medieval traditions of negative theology deserves particular attention. For though there are many forms of medieval heresy, some of which show so-called "mystical" tendencies, few draw upon so exclusively traditional a set of sources and conceptual materials as does Marguerite. Hence, the second reason for taking an interest in the special circumstances of Marguerite's case is that among the many things distinctive of the *Mirror* is its character of being a very original, highly speculative, conceptually sophisticated, and deeply traditional exploration of the very idea of limits and boundaries, of the idea of the licit and the illicit itself. And it seems that a key reason why Marguerite was burned has to do with a combination of genuine intellectual unease at her daring speculations on this topic—an unease that could only have been reinforced rather than diminished by the manner in which she constructed her speculations out of recognizably traditional materials—and rather more political motivations having to do with Marguerite's association with the Beguines. But both these elements of motivation are complex, and their interactions doubly so; nor is either quite what it seems, as the two authoritative historians of the subject, Lerner and Lambert, attest.[13] Let us take these two elements in turn, starting with the political.

WHAT CAUSES THE TROUBLE?

Marguerite's spiritual teaching is not typically Beguine. It is, of course, hard to say what is typically Beguine by way of formal teaching on spiritual matters, and easier to indicate broad lines of common practice. The Beguines were always a movement, never an organization. They flourished mainly in northern Europe, where by the early fourteenth century there were many communities of these laywomen, living a common life under their own regime, independent of direct parochial or episcopal control, observing, in principle at least, the strictest rule of poverty as regards personal possessions, but as communities more or less economically self-sufficient. To go beyond this broad description of practice requires detailed study of particular Beguine communities in particular times and places. And the same ought to be said about Beguine spirituality. It therefore seems hard to generalize, but insofar as one may do so, Oliver Davies, following Langer, seems right to characterize the piety of late thirteenth- and early fourteenth-century spiritual women as predominantly visual and active, typically expressed in the experience of visions, the encouragement of empathetic styles of prayer suffused in an imagery of ecstatic and courtly love, and in practice a firmly Christocentric and often Eucharistic piety and occasionally some near-extreme forms of bodily mortification.[14] Beguine piety may seem, therefore, to be typically expressed in its espousal of distinctive ascetical practices, and if Eckhart's preaching of a hard doctrine of inner worth as against outer practices can be seen as in some degree intended as a corrective to what he saw as an attachment among pious Beguines to spiritual practices and pious ways, then Marguerite's writing, in this so similar to Eckhart's, can at least be seen as a departure from mainstream Beguine spirituality, if not as a consciously critical reaction to it.

For Marguerite's teaching, again like Eckhart's, is decidedly apophatic, Dionysian, complex and nuanced in its employment of the dialectical "negation of the negation," austere in imagery, elusive in its rhetoric, and concerned in every way like Eckhart's to exploit the limits and boundaries of what can be said, at times transgressing those boundaries, only at others to draw hyperbole back within the safe limits of the legitimate and the orthodox.[15] These are the rhetorical strategies of Eckhart, who may very well have been influenced, especially in his own vernacular sermons, by Marguerite's evident pleasure in such teasing rhetorical strategies.

Marguerite is able to combine a subtlety of dialectical sophistication that amounts almost to a flirtatious playfulness with the sure control that comes from her debt to a deeply traditional apophatic theology.[16] In a passage of the purest Neoplatonic rhetoric she works together the Augustinian language of "inwardness" with that of the Dionysian "negation of the negation": "If [the annihilated soul] did anything through her outer senses, this would remain outside her, and if God did anything in her, this would be him working in her, for his own purpose, and so also outside her. What she does no more burdens her than what she does not do; she has no more being in herself, having given it all freely without asking 'why?' She no longer feels doubt nor trust."[17]

Such teasing is but the rhetorical expression of the logic of the conventional apophatic dialectics: she negates negations, she aims at a spiritual condition in which exclusions are excluded and one "no longer" feels "doubt nor trust." And her theoretical command over that logic itself is equally traditional and assured. At the sixth and highest pre-mortem stage of spiritual progress, the soul encounters a "dark night [that] snatches a quick glance at glory," and "This night is no less than the Trinity itself, revealing his inner being to the soul . . . but the light of this divine knowledge takes away from her all awareness of God or of herself or of anything else,"[18] and in general, "The more the soul knows of the goodness of God, the more it knows that it knows nothing of it, which only God can understand."[19] Yet this "not-knowing" of God is the true knowledge of God, and for the "pure and enlightened [soul] it is no longer her seeing God and herself, but God seeing himself in her, through her and outside her, and showing her that there is nothing other than God."[20]

In any case, Marguerite's confident vernacular exploitation of the Latin traditions of negative theology seems unlikely, by itself, to have provided enough evidence of heretical doctrine. Nor, by itself, does her Beguine association provide sufficient explanation of the ferocity of the assault on her teaching. For there seems to be no evidence before the early fourteenth century of hostility to the Beguines taking the form of accusations of heretical teaching. Throughout the thirteenth century hostility more often than not takes two forms that have a bearing exclusively on Beguine practice: first, there are accusations, sometimes scurrilous and often manifestly unjust, of licentious sexual behavior, and second, there are more general expressions of hostility to their unregulated, semiautonomous way of life and organizational regime. In particular, of course, the latter was of concern to bishops and secular clergy. But there is evidence also that the more formally recognized new religious orders, especially the Franciscans, disliked the mendicant ways of Beguines and the itinerant ways of their male counterparts, the Beghards, as constituting a direct challenge to their hegemony in these fields of spiritual endeavor.

By the late thirteenth and the early fourteenth centuries it was clear, however, that the Beguines could not be fatally wounded by accusations of personal misbehavior: their popular reputations for holiness by and large rode too high. More serious charges were needed, charges that transcended in importance those of unworthy behavior; charges that were less transparently self-interested than those directed at their ecclesiastical independence; and charges of a kind that would be sustainable on more convincing evidence than either. In short, what was needed was a palpable Beguine heresy. In fact it was not until very shortly before Marguerite's own condemnation that the first formal associations of the Beguines with heresy, specifically with the heresy of the Free Spirit, were made—by Archbishop Henry of Virneberg in Cologne in 1307. But Henry's ploy is of some significance for our understanding of the reasons for Marguerite's condemnation, for it was principally for promoting ideas identified as those of the Free Spirit movement that she was condemned.

Here, the problem of how to control the Beguines met with a parallel but different problem of chasing down the Free Spirit heresy. Both Lerner and Lambert have examined closely the evidence concerning this so-called heresy, and they draw broadly the same conclusion, namely that it was in good part but a loosely connected complex of antinomian and semi-Gnostic ideas and attitudes, most of which have some currency in some quarters, but that, as the coherent body of beliefs that were condemned periodically in the late Middle Ages, it was largely the fabrication of those who condemned it. Lerner comments that the bull *Ad nostrum* of the Council of Vienne in 1311 "is the birth certificate of the heresy of the Free Spirit. . . . But as if it were in the theatre of the absurd, there is a birth certificate without it being fully clear whether there was any child."[21] Lambert goes so far as to say that *Ad nostrum* "helped create heretics to match the Bull."[22] And it is indeed hard to identify any work at all in which the complex of ideas condemned in *Ad nostrum* is promoted as such. It would, of course, be wrong to say that the heresy of the Free Spirit was nothing but a bogey, and neither Lerner nor Lambert says it; but it is true to say that the evidence of any organized and intentional movement espousing its supposed doctrines is very hard to find.

Nor is this simply a problem of our lack of evidence. For it seems that the evidence of a genuinely Free Spirit heretical movement was lacking also to fourteenth-century inquisitors, that they were as much faced with the problem of pinning this heresy down as we are. And yet the ideas summarized and put together at the Council of Vienne in 1312 were, in different forms and in different places and on different occasions, definitely in the air. The problem for an inquisitor is that he cannot grasp air, but only books. He cannot condemn an intellectual and spiritual atmosphere, or burn a tendency: he needs statements and propositions to condemn and combustible promoters of them, books and persons. And both of these, for the inquisitors of the early fourteenth century, were in discouragingly short supply.

The problem of identifying a satisfyingly heretical Beguine therefore met in the early fourteenth century with the problem of identifying a satisfyingly embodied Free Spirit heretic. And we can see how they met in a series of early fourteenth-century condemnations that associate, more or less tightly, the Beguines with the Free Spirit movement. The first such connection was made in 1307 by Henry of Virneberg, though, as Lerner adds, there is no actual evidence from Cologne of Beguines or Beghards being tried for Free Spirit teachings until after the Council of Vienne.[23] The second, less local condemnation to make this association was found in the two Bulls of the Council of Vienne, *Cum de quibusdam mulieribus* and *Ad nostrum*, particularly the latter, in which, as Davies points out, the censorious hand of Henry of Virneberg can be identified.[24] And *Ad nostrum* derives its account of Beguine doctrinal errors very largely from the *Mirror* of Marguerite Porete. Between Cologne and Vienne, of course, lies the case of Marguerite herself, and these three events, taken in conjunction, just begin to clear the fog surrounding the second, Marguerite's case.

For consider the predicament of the inquisitorial mind such as Henry of Virneberg's. He needs an embodied Free Spirit heretic and he needs a heretical Beguine. What better than a person who is both, a Beguine who can be plausibly accused of the errors of the Free Spirit, and beyond all that, also a woman? What matter if this woman is not typically Beguine in doctrine so long as she is, or at least once was, a Beguine and can plausibly be represented as a heretic? For what matters is that her *Mirror* conveniently lies at the point at which the trajectories of different aim and purpose intersect, targeting Beguines and pinning the Free Spirit heresy down. Of course, the best that can be said is that this could explain the persecution of Marguerite. We have no direct evidence, since there is nothing in the reports of her trial of either accusation in explicit form: she is mentioned neither as a Beguine nor as a Free Spirit heretic as such. But we have two powerful bits of circumstantial evidence that what attracted the Parisian inquisitors to Marguerite's case was the opportunity to associate the Beguines with the Free Spirit heresy in a single, spectacular show case.

The first is the enthusiasm with which this association was taken up subsequently by the opponents of the Beguines, first at the Council of Vienne, later in Cologne and Strasburg. The two bulls of Vienne aptly illustrate the shift in emphasis within the anti-Beguine interest. The first, *Cum de quibusdam mulieribus*, is the more moderate, allowing a distinction to be made between orthodox and heterodox Beguines and stopping short of outright condemnation of the movement as a whole. Nonetheless, even in this bull it is notable that the issue is no longer either organizational independence or licentious behavior, but doctrine, though again, there is no explicit association of the Beguines with Free Spirit ideas. *Ad nostrum*, however, is an altogether tougher, less sensitive document and makes that association explicitly, particularly accusing Beguines of promoting antinomian ideas. Moreover, it is fair to say that among the doctrinal errors associated with the Beguines are a number which are described in precisely the terms of the known propositions for which Marguerite was condemned: antinomianism of a form that appears to disparage the perfected soul's need for virtues and a parallel disparagement of the ordinary means of holiness: petitionary prayer, asceticism, good works, and the sacraments.

Within the next decade, German Beguine hunters, particularly in Cologne and Strasburg, picked up the hint and ran, largely ignoring, as Davies points out, the careful distinctions of *Cum de quibusdam* and preferring to act on the blunter condemnation of *Ad nostrum*.[25] So undiscriminating were some of these opponents of the Beguines that their persecution provoked subsequently a number of decrees calling for restraint, even one in 1317 from the hostile John of Durbheim, archbishop of Stras-burg, and another in 1319 from the more sympathetic Pope John XXII.

The second item of circumstantial evidence is too complex for more than an outline here and relates to the subsequent case of Meister Eck-hart. There are parallels between his case and Marguerite's, and Ruh and others have argued that they are actually connected historically. The case for a historical connection is in part unquestionable. What we do know for certain is that Eckhart was living in the Dominican house in Paris in 1311, during his second term as *magister regens* of theology at the Univer-sity of Paris. Living in that same house at the time was William Humbert, the chief inquisitor appointed to Marguerite's case. There can scarcely be any doubt that Eckhart learned from him of the events of Marguerite's condemnation and hardly less that he knew of the propositions that she was condemned for promoting. It is even possible that Eckhart was ac-quainted with the *Mirror* itself before its first condemnation in 1306. Ruh believed that Eckhart's own condemnation was provoked by explicit state-ments in solidarity with Marguerite's ideas in some of his vernacular ser-mons.[26] And even if Davies is right that Ruh's claim goes beyond the evi-dence it is at least highly plausible to suggest that some of Eckhart's more extreme statements gave the same hostages to fortune as had Marguerite's, and that through his own association with Beguine communities in Co-logne and Strasburg he must have known that he was laying himself open to that same identification of the Beguines with Free Spirit errors of which Marguerite had fallen foul some sixteen years earlier.[27] In any case there is little doubt that by the time of Eckhart's trial, brought upon him by that same Henry of Virneberg who had campaigned for the harsh con-demnations of Vienne, the strategy of merging into one compendious ob-ject of persecution the two objects of hostility, the Beguines and the Free Spirit heresy, was a complete success. And it seems reasonable to think that the determination of the inquisitors in the case of Marguerite Porete was motivated by the opportunity she provided to bring those two issues together. Hers was too good an opportunity to be missed.

In summary, Marguerite's at least passably orthodox work met in its reception with a complex political web of ecclesiastical interest. Enmeshed in this web, her *Mirror* is necessarily situated within the contemporary perceptions of what was permissible doctrinally, but the issue of what was orthodox became entangled with a multiplicity of factors of ecclesiastical politics that interacted with one another, in very particular and contingent circumstances, to make her condemnation in 1310 especially opportune. First, there were factors of episcopal control, which for more than a century the unregulated life of Beguines had appeared to challenge; second, there were factors of contestation between the mendicant regulars, with whom for these purposes the Beguines and Beghards could conveniently be identified, and the secular clergy—a sore point throughout the thirteenth and fourteenth centuries; third, there were factors of rivalry and jealousy between the friars themselves and the Beguines, who were thought of as competing unfairly in the same mendicant market, which explains why prominent Franciscan theologians, like Nicholas of Lyra, could engage enthusiastically in the harassment of Marguerite. And then other Franciscans lay behind the prosecution of the Dominican Eckhart.[28] Finally there were genuine fears of the heresy of the Free Spirit. All these found their focus in Marguerite at a juncture when a focus of this congeries of hostilities, rivalries, and fears was needed. Marguerite had too many enemies to be safe, too few friends with an interest in protecting her.

WHAT DID SHE TEACH?

All these factors contribute, without doubt, to the case for explaining the *Mirror*'s condemnation in terms of realpolitik, given its being, on the doctrinal face of it, an implausible one. But there is more to be said, for the reason I have already given. Beguines disturb the late medieval mind because institutionally they disturb a pattern of boundaries within the ecclesiastical structures of late medieval society. Their way of life does not fit. Over and over again the complaint is that they are irregular. And in this context we may see the accusations of sexual licentiousness, unfounded as they appear to have been, more as a metaphor for that institutional irregularity than as either being based on real evidence or as being motivated by malicious slander. But Marguerite disturbed the early fourteenth-century mind for a more radical reason than that as a Beguine she represented this institutional disruption of order. She seemed to pose an ideological threat, for she appeared to be engaged, in a way that the majority of Beguines could not be represented as being engaged, in the revision of the very idea of boundaries: she seemed to challenge, not just the place where the boundaries of belief were conventionally fixed, but the very idea that they had fixity. In short, some of her more extreme theological statements seemed not only to be out of control but to cast doubt on the very idea of control, seeming to place hyperbole itself beyond the reach of sober doctrinal judgment. This, essentially, is what the charge of "antinomianism" consists in; this, in the end, is what the metaphor of "libertinism" is the sexual metaphor of; this is what "Freedom of Spirit" means, the breaking of intellectual bounds in principle, denying not the order of things but that in the end there is any order at all. This is the challenge that she seemed to throw down. But did she? And if she did not, why did she seem to?

To be fair to Marguerite's inquisitors, they deserve at least some sympathy. Nothing is easier in principle than to distinguish between the rule breakers who do homage to the rules they break and subversives who deny the rules themselves. The former is a conservative, a parasite, as is the thief who needs private property if there is to be any possibility of burglary at all, never mind of his profiting from the theft of it; or as is the adulterer whose thrills get their frisson from the marriage bonds transgressed. The burglar and the burgled have a common interest in property; the adulterer and the cuckolded spouse a common interest in marital fidelity. But the subversive subverts the complicity between burglar and burgled, between adulterer and cuckold. The communist approves neither of thieving nor of property; she says it is the property that is the theft. The advocate of free love scorns both fidelity and adultery because she scorns marriage. And so the common heretic, who needs the boundaries of belief in order to make the point of crossing them, is not to be identified with the radical, who challenges the boundaries of belief themselves. To the orthodox believer, therefore, there is comfort in the knowledge of common heresy, consolation in the heretic's acknowledgment that the perception of boundary is shared. But the radical bewilders because she denies the accepted terms of judgment. Nothing is easier than to distinguish these two in principle; and there is little that is harder to be sure of in practice.

For that reason, if the generalization may be risked, in perhaps every age the hunters of subversives have a common interest in denying the distinction in principle. Revolutionaries must be cast as common criminals. Terrorists must be denied their subversive potential by their redescription as common murderers. Those who challenge the church's authority as such must be tried as common heretics on points of particular doctrine. And the device of the medieval inquisitor most commonly used to contain the subversive potential of heresy was the gobbetizing of their errors, the compiling of lists of erroneous propositions for examination and rebuttal.

It is possible that historians today are themselves too easily distracted by this device. For on the whole, the inquisitors were successful—as Lambert says, the history of medieval heresy is the history of failure.[29] And it is the very success of the inquisitors that has left the modern historian with the problem of evidence, for generally we possess evidence of heretical teachings mainly from the gobbetizing documents in which they are condemned. We lack firsthand sources because they were suppressed. Therein is another reason why Marguerite is so important to us, for in this respect by historical accident we are fortunate: we possess the *ipsissima verba*. In spite of this, as I say, the historians may be misled, as they are if they suppose that what mattered to the inquisitors can necessarily be extrapolated from the gobbetized propositions they condemned.

Of course it is the common opinion of scholars today that the condemnation of the *Mirror* was ill-judged and unfair. The consensus of Lerner, Lambert, Davies, McGinn, and Babinsky is that the *Mirror* indeed contains statements capable of a heterodox interpretation, but all agree that it contains qualifications of those statements which, when all taken together, show even the more extreme statements to be capable of an orthodox interpretation. This does not really get to the heart of the problem, however, because although what William Humbert targeted was a set of fifteen suspect propositions lifted out of the context of the *Mirror*'s overall argument, it is reasonable to suppose that what chiefly worried him was less the propositions targeted as such than the tendency of the book as a whole. But the way to get at the book as a whole was to condense it one-sidedly into a set of recognizable, and pretty conventional, heretical statements. For this reason we need not take it for granted that it was those fifteen propositions themselves which were the motive for Marguerite's trial, though the thirty Parisian masters who were asked by Humbert to judge as to her orthodoxy naturally found unanimously against them. But it is arguable that that was the point of William's strategy—as we might put it, to reduce the subversive orthodoxy of the book as a whole to the level of conventional heresy.

Because she remained silent at her trial we can only guess at Marguerite's attitude to this procedure. She can hardly have been sympathetic. Eckhart, when subjected to similar treatment, made his attitude plain. He protested that though he held many of the opinions objected to by the Cologne inquisitors, in context they were sound; and for the rest, they were misrepresented in the versions submitted for his trial, for "even learned and studious clerics take down what they hear frequently and indiscriminately in a false and abbreviated way,"[30] as he put it diplomatically. And when presented with a later list of excerpts he complained that "just like the earlier ones, [they] are always or almost always false in the sense in which my opponents take them, but reasonably and devoutly understood they contain excellent and useful truths of faith and moral teaching."[31] Eckhart was all too familiar with the distorting effects of this procedure on judgments of orthodoxy, having witnessed, he notes, the same gobbetizing posthumously practiced on the recently canonized Thomas Aquinas— now, as he tartly points out, "given approval, both at Paris and also by the Supreme Pontiff and the Roman Curia."[32]

It is probable that Marguerite shared this view of this procedure. At any rate, an interrogation on statements ripped out of their context could hardly have seemed to her a fair way of conducting an examination of her opinions, in view of the manner in which she herself in the very structure of the *Mirror* conducts a searching and intellectually honest inquisition of her own into the orthodoxy of her theology. For the *Mirror* is constructed in the form of a conversation mainly between three participants, the Soul, Love, and Reason. The Soul (often herself) seeks to know ultimate truths, Love (who is God) answers sympathetically, and Reason (the church) poses objections to Love's answers. In the course of this three-way debate, Marguerite draws out a distinction that was bound to provoke, between Holy Church the Great and Holy Church the Less, the former consisting in the community of "liberated" or "annihilated" souls—souls, that is to say, who are perfected in the service of Love—and the latter constituted by those who live in the service of Reason. Now the precise nature of this distinction is less than clear in itself, though broadly the followers of Holy

Church the Less represented by Marguerite's Reason are those who live a life regulated by the disciplines of the virtues, the conventional practices of prayer, asceticism, and the sacraments, whereas the followers of Holy Church the Great have reached a higher condition of spiritual achievement, superior to any that can be reached by those conventional means, a condition of complete "annihilation" of self and of abandonment to love. What does seem clear is that the distinction is, in the first instance and throughout the *Mirror* principally, a moral distinction, that is to say between two qualities or levels of achievement of Christian life. What is less than clear, troublingly no doubt to church authorities, is the bearing the moral distinction had on the actual church as institution. Was Marguerite saying that the annihilated soul had no need of the institutional church, its prayers and sacraments, its penances and charitable works?

Frustratingly, but tellingly, she answers, "Yes" and "No." The annihilated soul does not depend on such common practices. But neither may she abandon them. She is free of them only in the sense that she is able to use them freely. Marguerite seems to taunt Reason with ambiguity on this question: she concedes that those who live by virtue, the sacraments, and the ordinary means of grace and good works, that is to say, by Reason, can be saved and are good. But she is at best condescending to the claims of Holy Church the Less and at worst appears to doubt whether it has any future.

But if Reason represents a lower way, one that cannot by itself lead to perfect annihilation of soul and union with God, the way of Reason is no easy path, nor does Marguerite cheapen the distinction between the Greater and the Lesser Churches by representing it as that between perfect and corrupt souls. Reason concedes that liberated souls are "in a life higher than ours, because Love dwells in them, whereas Reason dwells in us. But this does not go against us. Indeed, in our glosses on scripture we commend and praise [such souls]."[33] And when Reason has the opportunity to describe the Christian life she represents, it is no caricature that is offered but a full account of a demanding ascetical practice. "I give counsel," she says, "to the best effect that I know how to give," namely

> that [she] should desire contempt and poverty and every kind of trial, [desire] masses and sermons, and fasting and prayers and that

she should be cautious of every kind and manner of love, on account of the dangers that are possible there. And that paradise should be desired above all and that every kind of honor should be rejected along with every kind of worldly preoccupation and every carnal pleasure, in always depriving nature of what it demands, with the exception of that without which life is impossible, according to the example of patience and austerity of our Lord Jesus Christ.[34]

To which Love replies,

You are very wise and completely right about the things that are yours ... and I will reply to all your questions. I can confirm that those souls which are driven by the purest love, hold it to be all the same to them and desire equally shame as honor and honor as shame, poverty as much as riches, riches as much as poverty, to be tried by God and his creatures as much as to be consoled by them, and they desire to be hated as much as loved, loved as hated, hell as much as heaven, heaven as much as hell, a lowly condition and humble as much as a high and exalted one. ... These souls neither desire nor do not desire anything of the aforementioned outcomes, whether of good or ill fortune, for these souls have no will, except that God should will in them.[35]

It seems clear from this and other passages which we will consider shortly that though Reason may feel cut out by Love, Love's view of their relationship is inclusive rather than exclusive. Everything Reason demands Love concedes, but freely, not *as* demanded. Whereas Reason is bound by its practices of piety and good works, Love performs them entirely as a matter of Love. Whereas Reason is a slave to its obligations, Love fulfills in freedom all that Reason requires in obedience. Even Reason concedes that this is so, for whoever has the two strings of faith and love in her bow "has everything and has permission to do whatever pleases her, as is witnessed by Love itself, who says to the soul: 'Soul, Love and do what you will.'"[36]

Moreover, in spite of her claims to superiority over Reason, Love takes the objections Reason poses to her more daring claims with very great seriousness.

LOVE:
Once a soul has reached this state [of annihilation], she can say to the virtues: "I have no further need of you, now I have served you all this time."

THE SOUL:
I agree, dear Love. I was their servant, but your kind courtesy has set me free from enslavement to them. Virtues, I leave you behind forever! My heart is now freer and more at peace than it has ever been. It was hard work being your servant, that I know well. For a time I put my heart inseparably into your service and you knew it: I was completely given over to you, therefore then I was your slave, but now I am released, and I wonder how I was able to escape.

LOVE:
This soul knows no care, has neither shame nor honor, neither poverty nor riches, neither joy nor sorrow, neither love nor hate, neither hell nor heaven.

REASON:
For God's sake, Love, what are you saying?

LOVE:
What I mean can be understood only by those to whom God has given understanding and by none other; it is not taught by scripture, nor can human reason work it out. . . . It is a gift received from the Most High, in whom all knowing leads to loss of understanding. . . . So this soul that has become nothing possesses all and possesses nothing, knows all and knows nothing, wills everything and wills nothing.

REASON:
Lady Love, how can this be, you said before that this soul has no will? How, then, can she will everything and will nothing?

LOVE:
Because, dear Reason, it is not the soul's will that wills, but God's will willing in her; the soul does not rest in love as if led to it by any desires of her own. Rather, love rests in her, takes over her will, and has her will of her. So now love can work in the soul without the soul's will, and the soul will be freed from all cares.[37]

Leaving aside, for the moment, the potential in what Love says for an antinomian depreciation of the virtues (it is little enough in any case), we should attend to the fact of the dialogue itself. Love instructs the Soul about its condition of "annihilation." The Soul agrees, but Reason protests, first requiring an explanation of what Love means and then posing the objection that if the annihilated soul wills everything and nothing, how can she be said to have a will at all? A little later, Reason takes the objection a step further, arguing that if, as Love has explained, the soul has no will of her own, but only wills with the divine will, then to have taken leave of the virtues will leave her without any assurance of salvation, a prey to self-deception and illusion.[38] To which Love replies: "Absolutely not so. A soul of the kind we are speaking of has all the virtues and more truly has them than those inferior to her, but she does not have the use of them, because she does not *pursue* them as she used to. Certainly, she so fully served them that now she is worthy to possess complete liberty."[39] Hence, "This soul no longer knows how to speak of God, for it is annihilated and made insensible of all exterior desires, of every interior feeling and of every desire of its spirit. And so this soul does what it does out of the practice of good habits, or out of regard to what the church commands, without any desire of its own, for that will is dead in it which gives rise to desires."[40]

There is no doubt that Reason's objections are serious, need answers, and get them—nuanced, clarifying answers. The debate between Love and Reason is genuine, no mere formality. And if we take it that for Marguerite Reason represents the visible church of her times, then we can see that, regret as we must the loss of detailed records of her trial, the loss in one way is not so great after all. For in a very real sense the *Mirror* not only contains the materials that were judged at that trial but is, in its dialogic and dialectical structure, an idealized version of her trial by anticipation. It seems not entirely fanciful to suggest in this connection a reason why Marguerite remained silent when confronted with William Humbert in 1310. Marguerite had already faced every objection that Holy Church the Less could pose and had answered them all. As far as she was concerned, the trial had already taken place and there she stood acquitted by Holy Church the Great. If in the event the book did not defend itself, there could be no point in her trying to defend it.

It is possible that William, who no doubt had read the whole text of the *Mirror*, knew this, knew, that is to say, that because Marguerite had anticipated the judgment of her work in her own self-trial, the wind had been

taken out of the sails of his trial of it. The members of the Parisian theological panel who had only William's excerpts on which to pass judgment
could not, of course, take her own defense into account. But in fact there is
nothing in the *Mirror* judged heretical by the Parisian theologians, nothing
condemned at Marguerite's trial, nothing anathematized in *Ad nostrum*, to
which an objection is not raised by Reason and answered or explained by
Love within the *Mirror* itself. And it may therefore seem reasonable to suggest that it is that fact which William found so subversive that he could respond to it only by extracting propositions which in their isolation from
their dialectical context become indefensible, though in context they are
precise and are at least capable of being construed in an orthodox sense.

WERE MARGUERITE'S TEACHINGS HERETICAL?

Turning then to the question of the *Mirror*'s orthodoxy when taken as a
whole, of course no judgment could be based on the brief extracts I have
just quoted. Nothing but the sort of detailed theological and historical-
critical analysis that William never carried out on the whole text would
suffice for this purpose. In the meantime we can at least turn to the judgment of those medieval readers in the decades soon after Marguerite's execution who knew nothing of the *Mirror*'s history of condemnation, or of its
association with Marguerite, and found it not seriously wanting on point of
doctrine. And as for the orthodoxy of these last passages, they raise two central issues, one theological-doctrinal, the other ascetical practical.

As to the first, Marguerite's contemporaries should very well have
been able to perceive, and perhaps did perceive, that the debate between
Reason and Love would do passably well as a précis of well-known medieval debates about the theological or "infused" virtue of charity and
about the role of the Holy Spirit in infusing it. And they may very well have
drawn the conclusion, which we may draw today, that Marguerite's doctrine of Love and will goes no nearer to the limits of orthodoxy than do
those of the unimpeachably orthodox William of St. Thierry and Peter
Lombard,[41] both of whom had argued nearly two centuries before Marguerite that charity in the perfect soul is an uncreated reality, and in fact is
none other than the Holy Spirit itself, dwelling in the created soul. For
"[A] man's life is the love of God," said William, and "This is conceived by

faith, brought forth by hope, formed and endowed with life by charity, *that is the Holy Spirit.* For the love of God, or the love that *is* God, the Holy Spirit, infusing itself into man's love and spirit, attracts him to itself; then God loves himself in man and makes him, his spirit and his love, one with himself."[42] If we set this alongside Marguerite's formula, there is not much to choose between them. For Marguerite says no less, but equally no more than William: "*Love*: I am God, because Love is God and God is Love and this soul is God by reason of its love."[43] And if William can set such assertions against the qualifying background of the soul's being only by grace what God is by nature, so too can Marguerite, for Love, which is God, insists: "I am God by divine nature, this soul but by right of love."[44] Nor in Marguerite is this an incidental, merely conventional qualification, for she repeatedly insists upon it.[45] And if for Marguerite a soul annihilated by love, whose will is firmly fixed in the Trinity, "can no longer sin unless she can unfix it," since "there is nothing she can sin with" (sin being a product of the will and her will being "in the Trinity"), William says no less—in fact he expresses himself rather more unguardedly than does Marguerite: "Just as God is what he is, so the disposition of the good will in regard to the good of virtue is so firmly established in the good mind and impressed on it in its ardent clinging to unchangeable Good, *it seems wholly unable to change from what it is.*"[46]

On the other hand Reason's objections to this doctrine are no more the carping weasel words of a narrow orthodoxy than are the very similar objections of Thomas Aquinas to Lombard's teaching, since Thomas, like Marguerite's Reason, maintains that charity in the soul cannot be the Holy Spirit itself and can only be a created virtue in the soul, or else the human will is simply displaced and made irrelevant.[47] For, Thomas says,

> The work of charity does not issue from the Holy Spirit to move the human soul in such a way that the human mind is only the object of her action of moving and in no way the source of its own movement— as is the case with a body moved by an external mover. For this would be contrary to the very notion of a will, whose source of agency has to be within itself . . . and so it would follow that to love would not be a voluntary act. And that would imply a contradiction, since love by definition is an act of will.[48]

Thomas's objection to the teaching of William and Peter Lombard scarcely differs from the objection Marguerite's Reason puts to Love's version of it. It is a serious objection, and Marguerite treats it seriously, carefully nuancing her position in the face of it, so as to make plain her denial that the annihilated human will is identical *in nature* with the divine will, even if it is identical *in what and how it wills.* Her problem is, of course, one of consistency, but this is a problem she shares with the indubitably orthodox William of St. Thierry and Peter Lombard and is no more acute in her case than in theirs. Moreover, as Thomas himself shrewdly points out, the problem, though without question substantive in its consequences, is to some degree and in some cases no more than linguistic, or at least is unnecessarily obscured by rhetorical, not doctrinal, factors. It is a characteristic of Platonist traditions of discourse, he says, to describe in essentialist ways that which is intended participatively, to say that that is essentially such and such when what is meant is that it participates in that thing. Hence it comes naturally, if misleadingly, to the Neoplatonic mind to say that charity in the created soul is divine love when what is meant is that charity in the created soul participates in divine love.[49] And in Marguerite's case, Thomas's comment appears relevant. If she does say that the annihilated soul has no will of her own but loves by the divine love, she is also ready to say, with whatever consistency is another matter, that what in God is divine by nature is in the created will divine only by the *gift* of love.

So understood, Marguerite's doctrine of the soul's having no will of its own is at least capable of being represented as an orthodox, if also controverted, contribution to a well-known debate. Perhaps it is most naturally read in those terms. And if Marguerite's more learned medieval readers could have had little difficulty in recognizing the main lines of that ancient debate to have been compendiously reflected in her *Mirror,* it would be surprising if William Humbert had failed to recognize them too.

As to the second, ascetical-practical issue, that of the relation between love and the virtues, Marguerite appears to have effected a dramatic transposition of the Neoplatonic negative dialectics of language and intellect on to the whole field of human affect and desire.[50] The consequence is that what in the pseudo-Denys is the annihilation and self-transcendence of understanding in the darkness of the Godhead becomes also in Marguerite the annihilation of will in a total detachment of spirit and selfhood, a move that is productive of what may be called an apophatic anthropology corresponding with the traditional apophatic theological epistemology of the pseudo-Denys. But if this is so, then just as in the pseudo-Denys the moment of intellect's negation has to be understood carefully in its dialectical relation with the moment of intellectual affirmation, so in Marguerite does the negation of will and desire have to be set responsibly against the background of the acquisition of the virtues, the cultivation of ordinary sacramental means, and the practices of prayer and mortification. In neither the speculative nor the ascetical-practical case does the negativity make sense without the affirmation. Therefore, just as in the pseudo-Denys theological negation both transcends and includes within its transcendence every affirmation of God, so in Marguerite the annihilated soul possesses all the efficacy of virtue within a condition of charity that transcends and transforms that virtue. Thus perfect charity in the liberated soul possesses all virtue and none of it *as* virtue, but as identity with the divine will. And this is at once coherent theology, traditional teaching, and what Marguerite unambiguously says: not that love justifies the transgression of the obligations of virtuous living but that love gives to the virtues all that they demand, living as freedom what the virtues live as obligation. This is not, even remotely, an antinomian dispensation from ordinary moral obligation, for the liberated soul does all that the virtuous person does, but does it as love.

In a strictly orthodox sense, therefore, the liberated soul no longer needs the virtues, does not need "masses and sermons, fasting and prayers," for she is no longer a needy slave to them but is their mistress: "Such souls . . . more truly possess the virtues than do any souls which are lower than they, although they may not have the use of them, for these souls do not serve the virtues as they once used to," given that what was once the servant has become the mistress.[51] It does not follow from this that the soul does *not* pray, attend masses, mortify herself, and act virtuously.

Once again, therefore, Marguerite may be said to have pushed the language of the traditions of negative theological dialectics to the extreme limits, and it drives her into a kind of poetic hyperbole, while at the same time engaging, through the dialogic exchanges with Reason, in the conceptual and theological self-critique that demonstrates the logic within which that hyperbole is contained. Marguerite's strategy appears to be twofold: on the one hand she deliberately and, as I have said, teasingly, breaks the bounds of traditional theological discourse; on the other hand she employs the traditional apparatus of apophatic dialectics in order to demonstrate that the discourse self-subverts. On the one hand disruptive, on the other precisely controlled, her *Mirror* toys with the boundaries of language and belief while at the same time remaining firmly set within the traditions of apophatic theology that she inherits. And as it is centrally about linguistic self-subversion, so, as McGinn says, this "strange disappearing book" also does what it says,[52] for it subverts also itself: it is language in hot pursuit of the transcending defeat of language.

It was perhaps this contrived ambivalence that made the *Mirror* so hard a pill to swallow as a text. Combined with this ambivalence of language was the fact of its having been written in the French vernacular, the fact of its female and Beguine authorship, the fact that its argument steps outside the bounds of a first-level personal piety into the heady conceptual air of reflective theological dialectics, and perhaps the fact that it appeared, through its dialogical character of self-critique, to have preempted the judgment of Holy Church the Less in the name of a greater authority. The provocation of the *Mirror* was therefore in its whole tendency. Virtually everything about the *Mirror* represented danger, including, or perhaps especially, its capacity to be read as orthodox. Hence the inquisitor's need to gobbetize, hence the reduction of its complex theological subtleties to the platitudes of a conventional, condemnable, heresy. If this is right, then the *Mirror* was condemned not because it was seen to be heterodox, nor in spite of the fact that it was orthodox, but because its surface orthodoxy was, in the contingent junctures of early fourteenth-century ecclesiastical politics, more subversive than any straightforward heresy could ever have been. Perhaps what William Humbert perceived was that it was safer to condemn the *Mirror* as heterodox than to concede the subversive potential of its orthodoxy. And such a perception would not be all that surprising. For the year 1310 was not the first time, nor Paris the first place, in which the greater threat to the church was perceived to be, not after all heresy, but the demand that it adhere to its own orthodoxies, and that especially when the demand was made by a laywoman, a "fake woman," a *pseudo-mulier*.

The "Uniting Wisdom of Love"

The Story of a Late Medieval Controversy

Three chronologically overlapping late medieval "mystical writers" (as we call them today) figure in the short narrative of an exchange about the knowledge and love of God in the early fifteenth century. One is a giant, Jan van Ruusbroec; one a censorious gadfly, Jean Gerson; and the third is nowadays largely unknown, or at least unread, Denys the Carthusian, who said that, after the Pseudo-Dionysius, Ruusbroec was his favorite author, deserving of the name *divinus*.[1]

The story line is of a controversy, and the issue concerns how to describe the oneness of the soul with God that the love of God in this life draws the lover into. And concerning this, all three of our dramatis personae agree as to the fact: the summit of the Christian life is the perfection of divine love. What they disagree about is what that union of knowledge and love allows you to say of the identities of the lover and the beloved. In short, the question is whether those identities are lost in the abyss of love's uniting power, or whether those identities are rather retained and affirmed in it. And the story goes in summary something like this.

Gerson, writing in the early fifteenth century, thought that Ruusbroec, writing in the late fourteenth, had misconstrued that union of the soul with God in a manner which placed him in the company of the Free Spirit heretics; Denys the Carthusian, writing some twenty years after Gerson, responded that Gerson had misconstrued what Ruusbroec said, or at least what Ruusbroec plainly meant. I, for my part, think that Gerson and Denys in their opposed judgments of Ruusbroec's theology both miss the point and that in our plot it takes a fourth character at the beginning of the four-teenth century, Meister Eckhart, and a fifth in the mid-fifteenth, Nicholas of Cusa, to tell us why.

The bare story line of the disagreements between Ruusbroec, Gerson, and Denys is fairly quickly told,[2] though I shall tell it more briefly than will do full justice to all the nuances. What is more interesting is the why, and that will occupy me for the greater part of this chapter, though I might as well spoil the plot altogether by telling you here and now what I con-clude: that Gerson and Denys give us opposed misreadings of Ruusbroec for one and the same reason, namely that both have lost grip of an ac-count of the relation between identity and difference in the description of the soul's union with God of which Ruusbroec had a firm practical grasp, and of which Eckhart and Nicholas of Cusa knew the theology well.

GERSON'S CRITIQUE OF THE *SPIRITUAL ESPOUSALS*

In 1426, toward the end of his life, Gerson responded in two letters to a Carthusian prior, Brother Bartholemew,[3] who had written to Gerson wor-ried about the orthodoxy of Ruusbroec's principal work of mystical the-ology, his *Spiritual Espousals.* Gerson was put in a bit of a quandary by Bartholemew's query, being caught between a rock and a hard place. In Ruusbroec's own lifetime and for some time after his death in 1381, Car-thusians had on the whole been earnest supporters of Ruusbroec's repu-tation,[4] and Gerson, who liked the Carthusians almost alone among the monastic orders, could not abide Ruusbroec. Gerson was therefore par-ticularly keen to deflect Carthusian support from Ruusbroec's reputation and by and large succeeded. And that brings us to the third party to our historical debate, Denys the Carthusian. By the 1440s, when Denys was writing one of his own central works of mystical theology, *De contempla-*

tione, Gerson's influence on the Carthusians had already contributed decisively to the antispeculative bent of Carthusian piety, which, like some other late medieval spiritualities, was now distinctly hostile to the sort of daring speculations that had characterized the fourteenth-century Rhineland schools, as represented among others by Ruusbroec, Tauler, Suso, and, of course Meister Eckhart. Denys, an enthusiast for Ruusbroec and an ardent supporter of the intellectualist tendencies of Rhineland mysticisms, was already in trouble with his order, vexing his superiors as he did with what they thought of as these inappropriately scholarly and intellectualist priorities.[5] In summary, then, Gerson had an interest in dissuading the Carthusians of support for Ruusbroec; Denys, a Carthusian supporter of Ruusbroec and in consequence in trouble with his superiors, had an equally strong personal interest in defending his own intellectual position via the rebuttal of Gerson's critique of Ruusbroec.

What worried Gerson most was the orthodoxy of the first few chapters of the third book of Ruusbroec's *Spiritual Espousals*.[6] He had no problem with the first two books, in which, he says, he "found many things said . . . that are safe and sound and offering testimony of sublime matters."[7] Not that Gerson will accept the opinion he has heard expressed that this work "was written by a simple and unlearned person and . . . that therefore it would seem to have been compiled . . . in a miraculous fashion and by means of divine inspiration,"[8] for the work as a whole reveals its author to have been a considerable scholar, the style is sophisticated, and, more conclusively, the third book contains material that is at least "uncertain" doctrinally or "even false," and such opinions cannot be attributed to the Holy Spirit.[9] In fact, the third part of *Spiritual Espousals*, Gerson says, "must be completely rejected and rescinded, since it is either ill-expressed or else openly contrary to and discordant with the doctrine of the holy teachers who have spoken about our beatitude."[10] More specifically, the doctrines of this third book are close in spirit and word to those of "the sect of the Beghards, who were condemned some time ago by the decree of the church"[11]—this seeming to refer to the decree *Ad nostrum* of the Council of Vienne in 1312, condemning the Beguines and Beghards for their espousal of "Free Spirit" heresies.[12]

The two great historians of medieval heresy, Lerner and Lambert, agree that the so-called "heresy of the Free Spirit" never formally existed, even in the early fourteenth century, at least in the organized shape of specific doctrines promoted by a coherent and self-conscious body— not by any sect and least of all by the Beguines or Beghards.[13] Lambert even goes so far as to say that "definitions in *Ad Nostrum* helped create heretics to match the Bull,"[14] and certainly our best evidence of what this heresy was thought to amount to is found almost exclusively in the official church documents that condemn it. On the evidence of the decree *Ad nostrum*, the doctrines that got called by that name were chiefly two: autotheism and antinomianism, the doctrines that the perfect love of God makes the soul to become indistinguishably one with God and that the soul thus perfected has no need of, or worse perhaps, has no use for, Christian virtue or devotional practice. In 1310 the French inquisitor William Humbert considered that both heretical doctrines were to be found in Marguerite Porete's *The Mirror of Simple Souls*.[15] He decreed that this *pseudomulier*, a "certain Beguine," was to be executed as a relapsed heretic,[16] and on June 1 of that year she was duly burned at the stake.

Gerson appears to know little of the detail of this history;[17] indeed, he appears to confuse these condemnations of Beguine heresy in 1310 and 1312 with a quite different condemnation in 1333 by theologians at the University of Paris of the views of Guiral Ot (and indirectly those of Pope John XXII) on the beatific vision.[18] But what mattered was that the mud of Free Spirit heresy discharged at the Beguines and Beghards in 1312 was still sticking in 1426, and Gerson is determined that some will attach to Ruusbroec. So he goes on: "As I think, this author was a near contemporary of [the Beghards] and it could be that it was expressly in order to counter his conceit about the beatific or contemplative vision—which he perhaps shared in common with many others at the time—that the decretal [Gerson does not say which] was issued which laid down that beatitude consists in two acts."[19] Above all it is the taint of autotheistic heresy that this hounder of fifteenth-century heresies detects in book 3 of *Spiritual Espousals*.

The author asserts in the third part of this work that the soul which contemplates God perfectly not only sees him by means of that light which is the divine essence, but actually is that same divine light. . . . He adds that the soul of the contemplative person is lost within the abyss of the divine existence so that it is beyond recovery by any creature. It is possible to make use of a metaphor for this—though it is not one employed by him—that a small drop of wine dropped into the sea is quickly mingled with it and changed into it.[20]

Of course the metaphor of wine losing its identity in water—not, as Gerson admits, Ruusbroec's own, but rather Gerson's gloss—has no less authority behind it than that of another century's chief hunter of heretics, Bernard of Clairvaux,[21] but this does not stop Gerson from exploiting what he thinks of as its heterodox implications, which are, of course, that, on Ruusbroec's account of it, the soul's union with God in perfect love and knowledge is such that its character as created is entirely lost in its absorption into the Creator. And, prima facie, Gerson has a point. He quotes Ruusbroec's words—or rather the Latin rendering of them from which I am translating: "In that emptiness of [God], the spirit loses itself in blissful love and receives the light of God with nothing mediating, and it ceaselessly becomes the very light which it receives."[22] Further, the perfection of love is such that "our created existence depends on the eternal existence and is one with it according to its essential existence."[23] "All those who are raised up above their created existence into the utmost heights of the contemplative life are one with this God-making light, indeed they are this light itself. Accordingly, through this God-making resplendence, they see and feel and discover themselves to be uncreated in their existence and in their life, and to be one and the same with the simple emptiness of the Godhead."[24] (In Gerson's judgment) even more outrageously, Ruusbroec says: "There, the spirit is taken up above itself and is united with God, and tastes and sees in the oneness of the brilliant abyss, where in its uncreated existence it takes possession of the immense riches which he himself is, in the manner in which God tastes and sees them."[25] Gerson comments: "You might suppose from the sound of these words that on such an account the soul ceases to exist in that mode which it possessed previously in its own kind, and is changed or transformed and absorbed into the divine existence, and flows back into that ideal existence which it had, from eternity, in the divine nature."[26]

If these formulas of the soul's union with God appear to negate the distinction between Creator and creature, they must in consequence obliterate the individual identity of the person. For if matters stood as

Ruusbroec explains them, then, in the beatific vision in heaven the glo-
rified body would lose its own soul and

> would in [its own soul's stead] acquire the divine essence as that
> which formally gives it life—or else it would have no life at all; but in
> that case the soul would not be of the same kind as it was before, in
> fact it would have only that existence and life which it had from eter-
> nity in the divine art; and then the soul's bliss would consist in that
> manner of existence in which from eternity any soul, including the
> damned soul, [possessed] the divine life. For the human body in glory
> would not be able to recover its soul as its formal principle of life; or
> if it could the soul would not be annihilated in the way he says it is.
> And innumerable consequences, all absurd, would follow.[27]

There is no doubt that Ruusbroec says the things which Gerson believes entail these "absurd consequences," though equally there is no doubt
that Ruusbroec did not accept that his words did in fact entail them. But
that on the surface Ruusbroec's words were ambiguous to contemporary
readers, even to some more kindly disposed than Gerson, is shown by the
fact that Ruusbroec composed his later *Little Book of Clarification* in response to anxieties which Carthusian friends had expressed to him about
the orthodoxy of *Espousals*, book 3.[28] And it is very probably to the *Little
Book* that Denys the Carthusian appealed in his defense of Ruusbroec
against Gerson's polemic when he wrote his own work on contemplation.

DENYS THE CARTHUSIAN'S DEFENSE OF RUUSBROEC

"To be united with [God]," Denys says, "is to be lifted above oneself, it is to
fall and flow away from oneself, it is to be plunged into God, it is to expire
and die in him, it is to be absorbed into him so as to become one and the
same with him, it is to possess and draw upon that life which makes the
living person to be god-like, it is to be made divine by the most completely free gift of likeness."[29] For his part, Denys adds, he intends nothing
by this to imply "the destruction of created existence or its displacement,

or that [the person's] being is carried over into or transformed into the divine or 'ideal' existence, for it is in the nature of an elevation of the mode of existence, involving a qualitative change, of a very special and exceptional resemblance," one that, as he puts it, "forges between two wills a singleness of yea and nay,"[30] not between two existences a singleness of identity. Moreover, he insists, this is all Ruusbroec meant when he said "that we are to become one with God, one life, one happiness,"[31] clearly here paraphrasing the language of the *Spiritual Espousals*. Consequently, Denys goes on, "one author" (meaning, of course, Gerson)

> who attends to the surface meaning of [Ruusbroec's] words rather than what he intended, wrote that [Ruusbroec] proposed to revive the error of those who say that the rational creature, by virtue of his being raised up to God, returns to and is changed into his "ideal" and uncreated existence: which was a very vulgar and most crass error. It should not be thought that this John [Ruusbroec] ever intended to make such a claim or revive it: in fact he wrote bitter words against this error. Nonetheless, his manner of speaking was often hyperbolical, as was that of certain other saints, in the excess of their devotion and the fervor of their charity.[32]

THE "MODUS LOQUENDI" OF THE PLATONISTS

Loyal though Denys's defense of Ruusbroec may be, it is, in my view, uncomprehending of the inner logic of Ruusbroec's thought. Ruusbroec's "hyperbole" is not the product merely of pious fervor, and in any case were it simply that, his account would still be vulnerable to Gerson's second level of critique, namely that Ruusbroec's intended meaning can be derived only from what he has actually written, so that even if he is let off the hook of explicitly heretical aforethought, his failure still lies in the manner of his expression, which piety cannot be allowed to excuse.[33] There is, in any case, more to it than that: the diagnoses of Gerson and Denys, opposed as they are, are equally superficial. What leads Ruusbroec to his hyperbolical formulas of the soul's oneness with God are pure necessities of thought and language, necessities that derive from the Neoplatonic soil in which Ruusbroec's theology is rooted. An earlier diagnostician of Neoplatonic thought, Thomas Aquinas, got very much nearer to comprehending this inner logic of Neoplatonism than did either Gerson or Denys, though his discussion relates to a different, if not entirely unrelated, issue.

That was the issue raised for him immediately by Peter Lombard's discussion of the status of the charity with which the soul loves God, for Peter, in this following William of St. Thierry before him, took the view that since God, and more specifically, the Holy Spirit, is charity, the love by means of which the Christian soul loves God *is* the Holy Spirit itself.[34] Thomas, in the *Summa theologiae* as also elsewhere, notes that it is Augustine's authority no less that is commonly appealed to in defense of this view. For Augustine in *On the Trinity* says that "God is said to be charity in the same sense in which he is said to be spirit."[35] Therefore, Peter's argument goes, "Charity in the soul is nothing created, but is God himself."[36] To which Thomas replies that of course it is true that the divine essence is charity just as it is wisdom and goodness. For this reason we do say that the good are good by virtue of the divine goodness and that the wise are wise by virtue of the divine wisdom, but this is because the goodness by which we are constituted as good is a kind of participation in the divine goodness, just as the wisdom that makes us wise is a sort of participation in the divine wisdom. It is in the same sense that the charity by which we love our neighbor is a sort of participation in the divine charity. But, he adds, participation is not the same thing as identity, though "this way of putting it is customary among the Platonists, by whose teachings Augustine was much influenced." There are, however, those who "are unaware of this and derive cause of error from his words."[37]

This does get nearer to the point, at any rate, of Thomas's own personal temperament, which is always to reduce the temperature of Neoplatonic expressions of erotic enthusiasm where he fears hyperbole will lead doctrinally astray. But let us allow erotic hyperbole a little space and note that it is not confined to deviant or even heretical mysticism of the fourteenth century. Gerson in his way, and Thomas in another, may not like it, but they do need to lump it, because hyperbole in all ages is the natural language of erotic love.

EROTIC HYPERBOLE

One has only to recall Emily Brontë's *Wuthering Heights*, and Catherine Earnshaw's conversation with Nelly in the kitchen. She loves Heathcliffe, Catherine insists, "not because he is handsome, Nelly, but because he is more myself than I am."[38] Just so for Augustine (and not, I think, on account of the Platonists), for whom God is "more within me than I am to myself."[39] "Whatever our souls are made of," says Catherine, "his and mine are the same."[40] So too John Donne, for whom

> When love, with one another so
> Interinanimates two souls
> That abler soule which thence doth flow
> Defects of lonelinesse controules.
> Wee then, who are this new soul, know,
> Of what we are compos'd and made,
> For th'atomies of which we grow
> Are soules, whom no change can invade.[41]

"But surely," Catherine goes on, "you and everybody have a notion that there is or should be an existence of yours beyond you. . . . Nelly, I *am* Heathcliffe. . . . He is always, always, in my mind—not as a pleasure, any more than I am always a pleasure to myself, but as my own being—so don't talk of our separation again—it is impracticable."[42] Just so another Catherine, of Genoa, reported in the early sixteenth century as having said the same, a simple and unapologetic "My being is then God."[43]

But do we need to say, as Thomas and Denys rather grudgingly do, that such hyperboles are no more than the understandable lift-off of an erotic, formally unjustifiable Platonist hyperbole, forgivable so long as one keeps one's conceptual feet firmly planted on the solid ground of Thomist realism?

I think not. It will not do justice to the case to say, as Thomas implies, that Neoplatonists use the predicate of identity in a merely rhetorical fashion when what they really mean is creaturely participation. For Platonists, the degree of a thing's existence *is* the degree of its participation in

The Existent. And this means in the first instance that a thing's identity as what it is lies in the degree to which it participates in its form, so that its "isness" as this or that is directly proportional to its participation in "what-it-is-to-be" this or that. And it means in the second instance that the extent to which a thing participates in its form is the extent to which it is the form it participates in. Whereas, therefore, for Thomas, a thing's participation in another entails its nonidentity with what it participates in, for the Platonist unqualified participation in another is identity with it. And what holds for this Platonism thus roughly characterized in general holds for Ruusbroec, for this is what his famous "exemplarism" amounts to. This is why Ruusbroec can say so emphatically what Gerson takes such exception to: "This eternal going forth and this eternal life which we eternally have and are in God apart from ourselves is the cause of our created being in time. *Our created being depends upon this eternal being and is one with it in its essential subsistence.*"[44]

Here, then, we get to the crux of the matter. "Our created being," says Ruusbroec, "... is one with [this eternal being] in its essential subsistence." But, we may ask, how both: how created if one with the Creator's being "in its essential subsistence"? Thomas, we may imagine, could resolve the paradox on the assumption that Ruusbroec did not really mean that creature and Creator are identical existentially, but only that an exceptional degree of participation is rhetorically misdescribed in those terms. Denys could and does put it down to pious hyperbole. But what if Gerson is right and Ruusbroec means what he says, particularly if what he says is so to be construed in Platonist fashion as to mean that the soul becomes one existent with God? What are we then to make of the apparent oxymoron: our created existence is one existent with the Creator's? And note that it will not be enough in Ruusbroec's defense merely to list the innumerable texts, whether in *Spiritual Espousals* itself or in the later and more consciously defensive *Little Book of Clarification*,[45] in which he makes clear that nothing he says about oneness with God should be taken as entailing the denial of the created identity of human persons. For that defense only intensifies the oxymoronic effect of saying both. In any case, the question is not whether Ruusbroec wants to say both things, for he constantly does, but how consistently he can say both things, for he clearly seems to think he can. How, in short, does Ruusbroec get away with affirming my union [with God] "without distinction" consistently with affirming my identity as a creature? Even more simply, how can you consistently say: Ruusbroec is one existent with God, Gerson is one existent with God, yet Ruusbroec and Gerson are two distinct created individuals?

That question brings us back to our senses, for the direction we have been moving in is exactly the opposite of where we should be going. When it comes to hyperbolic, if forgivable, talk about erotic oneness between lover and beloved, it is Catherine Earnshaw's "Nelly, I *am* Heathcliffe" that fills the bill, not Catherine of Genoa's "My being is then God." Catherine Earnshaw can only with forgivable hyperbole say she *is* Heathcliffe, because manifestly she is not: Catherine and Heathcliffe are distinct individuals in such a way that being the one excludes being the other, which is exactly what Heathcliffe himself dramatically demonstrates by abandoning Catherine apparently without a moment's hesitation, leaving her with all Donne's "defects of lonelinesse" uncontrolled. Catherine's being Catherine excludes her being Heathcliffe as any two created individuals must necessarily do.

But that is just what is not true of Ruusbroec, Gerson, and God. Ruusbroec and Gerson add up two individuals of a kind, two nonidentical human beings. Ruusbroec, Gerson, and God—do they, can they, add up to three, if they do not add up to three individuals of a kind? And if you say that they do add up to three, to three instances of what do they add up? The question is crucial: after all, Thomas himself is the first to know this, Ruusbroec and Denys the Carthusian know it, and only Gerson seems to have lost his grip on a key element of the logic of late medieval mystical theology. For the answer has to be as Thomas himself says: there is no list, not even (were one possible) the list of everything ever existent, to which you can add God as an additional item, as amounting to that sum plus one. God is not an *additional* anything, because, as the pseudo-Denys says, there isn't any kind of thing that God is, so that there is no kind of thing that God is an instance of, not even the one and only instance of it. God is not one anything. God can neither add to any list nor exclude anything from any list. God excludes nothing. I, and my individuality, however, exclude you, and yours.

Nicholas of Cusa later in Gerson's century puts the same point nicely in a quite unnecessarily opaque text, of which only the title is (for me) illuminating: *De ly-non-aliud*, or, as we might paraphrase, "On [God as] the one and only existent who is *not* 'other'"; and then there is Meister Eckhart saying that God's distinction from creatures consists in God's not being what all creatures necessarily are, namely distinct, as one thing is from another, for God is distinct by virtue of not being in any such way distinct. This is not head-in-the-air mystical hyperbole. It is the feet-on-the-ground logic of language about God, and it now thus adjudicates the late medieval debate.

Gerson has confused Ruusbroec's "The soul is one with God in his essential subsistence" with Catherine Earnshaw's "Nelly, I *am* Heathcliffe," a sort of sudden rush of metaphorical blood. But Ruusbroec and, in the end, both Thomas and Denys the Carthusian know better than to fall into that error. For all three can see that the problem of identity's excluding distinction cannot possibly arise here, in the relation between creature and Creator, as it does between one Catherine and another. For the two Catherines are distinct from one another or from Heathcliffe on ordinary, secular criteria for individual distinction, whether or not any or all of them are identical with God. And this is because their identity as individuals is a function of their distinction from one another. But if identity with God is not identity with another individual—as, God not being a distinct individual, it cannot be—then there is simply no possibility of construing that identity with the Creator as exclusive of my identity as a creature. For it cannot be the case that my identity as a creature is in any way constituted by, or is in any way dependent upon, my distinctness from God, in the way that my identity as a creature is constituted by my distinctness from other creatures. Hence, while there is not, and cannot be, any way positively of comprehending how my identity with God is consistent with my creaturely existence, there equally cannot be any way of construing them as inconsistent.

Hence, Ruusbroec can mean what he says: he can both eat his cake and have it. Nor only can he, he must, for his oxymoron is not a bit of overenthusiastic piety, or a Neoplatonic misdescription of a platitude, but a paradox demanded by the very necessities of theological discourse itself. We have to say both those things that, otherwise than construed in and through the dialectics of Neoplatonism, collapse into a logically incoherent babble—and, as Gerson thinks, into autotheistic heresy. I emphasize: the thing ends in that paradox. The oxymoron cannot be dissolved, there being no univocal description to dissolve it into, for if one point of that dialectics is to demonstrate that this paradox does not amount to gobbledygook, the other point of it is that a resolution is demonstrably indescribable, for here we are in the land of unknowing, of a love beyond love. If the two things we have to say are not inconsistent, nonetheless we do know that there are no terms in which their consistency can be demonstrated.

I suppose for some this will all seem like a reversal of the natural priorities. For we would probably be inclined to suppose that the starting point from which our language of the love of God must set out is going to have to be our worldly experience of love, which we then extrapolate upon, stretch out toward, exaggerate beyond all experience in the description of the love of God. And I guess that is so insofar as the *ordo inveniendi* is concerned (as Thomas would put it): for the way we come to know of the love of God is by means of our experience of creaturely love. But what is significantly odd about this is that the priorities are reversed in point of what love is. It is Catherine Earnshaw's "I am Heathcliff" that is love's hyperbole, love's speech as figurative and failing of literal truth. It is Catherine of Genoa's "My being is then God" that is literal and understated; it is the love that unites God and the soul in Ruusbroec's oneness with "the eternal being in its essential subsistence" that, far from hyperbolically overstating the case, falls infinitely short of anything we can comprehend. Gerson entirely misses the point. In fact his significance historically lies in his having missed the point, in his being one of the first to miss a point that, alas, we have not yet in our times seen the last theologian all too ready to do.

PART III

MYSTIFICATIONS

SEVEN

Why Is There Anything?

It was in the audience at a particularly uninspired performance by one of the Terry lecturers here in Yale—these being annual lectures endowed for the purposes of exchange between the scientific and theological disciplines—that Priyamvada Natarajan, professor of astronomy at Yale, and I met for the first time and agreed that there had to be a better way of doing things than that.[1] Not that we actually knew how to do better. On the contrary, we were both deeply puzzled by some of the questions that awkwardly poke their heads up through the spaces between science and religion, though we didn't know for sure if that was how best to put it, for maybe it wasn't the spaces between them—if there are any—where the best questions arose, maybe it was at their intersections as they happen to cross over while on their separate ways elsewhere, or perhaps it was in their overlaps on some common ground, or even at points of conflict between them. We had no certainty as to in which of these connections the most creatively helpful questions arose, though we did share the feeling that too many of the attempts we knew of to get a conversation going between scientists and theologians seemed dominated by people who were just a shade too certain of themselves and insufficiently puzzled by such questions. On both sides were those who knew where they stood themselves, whatever about where the others stood, and that was pretty much that. They were unlit ships, relative positions unplotted and trajectories not calculated, passing one another in a starless and moonless night.

At any rate, that was most definitely the case when it came to the issue that has (in my view most unfortunately) come to dominate the debate between scientists and theologians, even to the point of there being a real-world politics entangled with it in the United States, namely the arguments about how the evolution of species by random natural selection stands in relation to Christian beliefs about creation and divine providence. Priya and I immediately agreed that a pox would best be visited on the unholy alliance between the houses equally of those evolutionary theorists, such as Richard Dawkins and Daniel Dennett, who think that evolution entails ditching God, and of their mirror-image fundamentalist Christians, such as Jerry Falwell, who maintain that you have God only at the price of ditching evolution.[2] For both parties seemed to be locked into one and the same fundamentalism. Priya and I thought we had better things to do with our time than re-engage in a debate that largely consists in cheap parodies on both sides.

On the other hand, I don't think any of the three of us who in due course got this conference going are very much interested in generalized discussions about science and religion just for the sake of them; such discussions are usually too much of a second-order character, with the consequence that the questions arising there are really no one's questions, occupying neither the scientist's nor the theologian's home intellectual territory. In short, they engage in too much inter- and not enough discipline. And so the idea began to emerge that we might get a different and more fruitful kind of debate going if we could identify an issue in which all parties had to be interested on their own terms, but that was situated at a point intellectually at which all were equally puzzled, equally unsure of themselves, even to the extent of being unsure as to whether the issue was real or bogus. We needed an issue that would be tempting enough for both scientists and theologians to have a go at, but one on which neither discipline had so many dogmatic axes to grind that, as with the evolution-versus-Creation issue, real debate was made impossible.

Thereafter it took no time at all to see that if we were going to attempt any such thing we needed the philosophers in on the game from the outset.

And so it was that another Yale professor, Michael della Rocca, signed up to the project early enough to prevent Priya and me from making some obvious conceptual mistakes in the initial formulations of the conference agenda that at this stage we were envisaging.[3] As academic advisers, all three of us were used enough to requiring our students when preparing semester papers to work hardest on getting clear about how to formulate a precise question, one to which their papers could then be constructed by way of an answer, that we decided to take a leaf out of our own teaching books and give the conference a title in the form of a question. Thus it was that we struck upon the title "Why Is There Anything?" as heading it up. It was, we thought, a question that, as it stood thus abstractly posed, was sufficiently malleable to the purposes of our three disciplines of cosmology, philosophy, and theology, while still occupying enough common ground of ordinary meaning that our separate responses might not become entirely lost in the translation between them, and that also, as puzzling questions go, seemed about as puzzling as they get.

And with that question in place, I was about to say we imagined that, as with the student semester papers, we would be in a position to structure the conference agenda out of considerations relevant to answering it, each as our respective disciplines required, and that then we could spend time comparing notes. I was about to say that, because at first we thought that setting an agenda for this conference would be that straightforward. And, for all I know, it might be possible to hold such a conference if you carefully selected the right participants and, among other constraints, were sure not to invite any philosophers along to its sessions. But let philosophers in on it and if no one else did they would be sure to set squads of unherdable cats among the comfortably ensconced pigeons, because they would be bound to ask all sorts of second-order questions about the question "Why anything?" itself. And that, of course, was exactly the reason why we had known we had to bring the philosophers into it.

For the first thing to note about the question, indeed about any question that like ours begins with the interrogative "Why?" is that it has more than one meaning. For one thing, if by that question you imagine yourself to be asking about the antecedent conditions that must obtain if there is to be anything at all, the question prima facie sounds pretty nonsensical, because, presumably, those antecedent conditions are something, and so you would have to repeat the question "Why anything?" about those antecedent conditions too. And that is not so much to engage thought in an infinite regression—which is at least going on the move, and if nowhere in particular, still endlessly—as to not even be going at all, just spinning mindlessly on the spot, a whirring cogwheel disengaged from the machinery of thought.

But suppose you took the question "Why?" to interrogate not antecedent conditions but purpose, asking, to what end there is anything at all, what is it for? For myself, I cannot see how a question so formulated can make any better sense than the previous one, for questions of purpose have to be answered by way of demonstrating some fit, or the lack of it, between what you have got and what it is for. And of course asked just of anything at all regardless of what, questions of fit between what you have got and what it's for cannot be answered: you need values for the indeterminate "anything" before you can even set about trying to answer the question "Why?" asked as of its purpose. For if it is indifferently any old thing you are asking about, then it can be for any old purpose. Say what it is and then there is some chance that you can say what it is for, otherwise not.

At this point, when explaining what we had in mind as our conference topic, we would get impatient looks (when they were not just rather glazed) from people who could see no point in asking the question "Why is there anything?" but every reason for asking, concerning the universe we have actually got, "Why *this*?" Otherwise than thus narrowed it would seem that the question hangs too loose for any determinable strategy of answering to be capable of yielding an explanation. But if anything is clear about how to distinguish what the scientists are up to as distinct from what the philosophers and the theologians might be up to, then it is that the scientists own the question "Why this?" Answering it is their job, because they can organize a relation of fit between the meaning of that question and what you have to know in order to answer it, and they have ready to hand methods of inquiry that in principle, if not yet in fact, can yield the required knowledge. Naturally, they may not actually have the answers, but they know that, if anyone does, they are the ones who have what it takes to discover them. At any rate, they can safely make this claim, and make it as exclusively theirs, so long as the question "Why?" means "What are the conditions—perhaps the causal mechanisms—such that, given the description of an initial state of affairs, the outcome has to be what we have observably now got?"—or, as is the more usual explanatory state of affairs, the other way round: "What must the initial state of affairs and causal laws have been such that the universe is now as it is?"

There may be some theologians who, in a parallel strategy, would wish to maintain that, so long as what you are asking about is not "anything," but "this," the world that we have, then the question "Why?" is answerable in terms of that second meaning of "Why"—To what end do we have a universe like this? Speaking for myself I do not seem to have any academic friends in the theological world who think an answer is available to the question even so understood, but I do know there are some who do. Certainly I have listened to sermons by priests and others who are pretty sure that Christianity can and does provide exactly that: the answer to the question "Why have we got the sort of world that we have got?" and some Muslims of my acquaintance and some Jews make similar claims. A lot of atheists expect it of you. I was once asked by Jonathan Miller on a BBC television program why God would have created a universe in which it would take little short of 13.7 billion years before any creature evolved capable of knowing that it had taken little short of 13.7 billion years to get that far. It was as if he imagined that, as a Christian, I ought to have an answer, and he seemed quite upset to be told that I hadn't the first idea why that might be so, and that, speaking as a Christian, I don't think that Christianity offers anything of the sort that Dr. Miller was asking for. And then speaking as one whose thought is much influenced by Thomas Aquinas, I am further persuaded that what it is all for is entirely beyond us, even though, finally, I am of the belief that there is something that it is for. Hence, though I don't think we know the answer, I do think the question "Why this?" sensibly bears the meaning: "What is the purpose of the universe that we have?"[4]

So far so good, we thought, at least we had cleared some ground for our conference agenda, even if we did not yet know exactly what of substance would populate it. Or rather, so far, alarmingly bad for our conference's prospects. For the question that we seemed able to make sense of, or rather, two senses of, "Why this?" was not the question "Why anything?" that we wanted our conference to address. Worse than that, it was beginning to seem that our conference question had thus far wandered altogether off the map that plots intelligible relations between questions and public, standardized methodologies of answering them. Indeed, the question seemed to have emigrated beyond the borderlines of sense itself. As a result we began to wonder if we had not found ourselves by default boxed into the sort of corner that the logical positivists of the last century would have had us boxed into from the start, that there is only stuff and nonsense and since all you need for the handling of stuff is science, all the rest is nonsense. Were this how things stood, what Priya and Michael and I ought to have done would be to plan a conference on the question "What accounts for the world that we have got?" just for scientists, though Michael and I would have been redundant, except to encourage Priya from the sidelines while she and the cosmologists got on with the real job.

It is fair to say, then, that we were far from unaware of this possible response when, in defiance of positivist scruples, we decided to persevere in our determination to headline the conference with the question "Why anything?" and ask cosmologists, astronomers, philosophers, and theologians of every hue and stripe to engage with it, because we were not prepared to surrender in advance to the proposition that the question did not and could not make sense. Of course we not only knew that some of those we invited to be speakers were distinctly of the view that the question made no sense; we also knew that there were others who did not very much care whether it made sense or not, because either way it had no bearing on their work as scientists; but we did know that there were yet others who, like us, thought that it might help all sides to learn how to mind their language a little more carefully if we were to get together and agree to treat the question as open to interrogation by all of us, and to see what happened when we interrogated it. All we asked of you our colleagues was to come from all around the globe on one condition, namely that you did not take it for granted as beyond discussion that you had a question worth asking only when you knew that you had available to you standard routines for answering it. For that is dangerously close to the sort of methodological dogmatism that caused Cardinal Borromeo to demand of Galileo that he revise his astronomical calculations in line with pre-Copernican predictions as to the orbits of the planets: we *know* what counts as an answer, the theologian said to the astronomer, and yours does not count as one. It is no better now than it was then for the astronomers to turn the tables on the philosophers and theologians and rule out the question "Why anything?" on the grounds that the astronomers know what counts as a question and that the theologian's question does not meet the conditions.

So let us not rule out on some generic criterion, whether of meaning or of scientificity, the question "Why anything?"—at any rate not before making a fair and responsible interrogation of it. Now as to that, it is not the case that anything goes and that there are no rules, and it is certainly true that to silly questions you can get only silly answers, so it would seem fair to require of our question's having traction that you can in principle provide the answer to the further question: Given that there being something or other existent is some state of affairs, with what state of affairs does it contrast? For after all, if I am a geneticist, I can ask why such hair as Turner has is vaguely brown only if I know what states of affairs would correspond with its not being brown—its being red, or black, or going white, or just mainly no longer there at all. But therein lies the trouble with the question "Why is there anything?" For when you ask, "Anything as distinct from what?" the answer yields no description of a state of affairs—in fact it rules out any such description. For the only answer to the question "What does there being anything contrast with?" is "nothing," and "nothing" is not the name of some state of affairs. You get a similar result from the consideration, as Christians, Muslims and Jews would have it, that God created the world *ex nihilo*, "out of nothing."

Grammatically, of course, the preposition *ex* in Latin, or "out of" in English, governs some noun or noun phrase descriptive of the material from which something is made—"out of wood," "out of tungsten," or whatever. And imaginations run riot here, seduced into fantasies by the misleading impetus of the ordinary grammar: if the universe is created out of nothing, then imagination would have it that here too there is some state of affairs called "nothing" and that the universe comes to existence out of it. This might seem to be too obviously nonsense to be worth mentioning, but I assure you that I have heard a physicist seriously claim to be happy with the Christian, Jewish, and Muslim doctrines of creation out of nothing, because (so I was told) there was indeed nothing antecedent to the Big Bang, only "random fluctuations in a vacuum." And in view of all such muddled nonsense it really is necessary to agree on some linguistic and conceptual discipline: simply put, when you speak of "random fluctuations in a vacuum" you may reasonably tell me that that is just a very odd way of not describing anything, and then I will accept that the phrase does not denote a state of affairs. But if you are telling me that "random fluctuations in a vacuum" is a physicist's description of what "nothing" is, then I will tell you that the physicist is no longer talking physics but just nonsense through a hat. Thomas Aquinas is quite right. The preposition *ex* in *ex nihilo* does not govern the description of some state of affairs out of which whatever there is has been created. Rather it is the negativity of the *nihilo* that governs the *ex*: here, in the creation of whatever there is, there is no out of at all, no initial conditions, no primal soup, not even the "formless deep" of the book of Genesis, and for certain no "random fluctuations in a vacuum." You may deny, almost certainly some will do so, that an act of creation so described occurred or even is possible. But at least get clear what it is you are denying if that is what you think you should do; and least of all should you think you are agreeing with any classical doctrine of creation, if you suppose creation to be the making of a universe out of something or other that answers to the description "nothing." Alas, there isn't anything that answers to the description "nothing," and certainly "random fluctuations in a vacuum" does not answer to it.

Having just said that in the view of the three of us who conceived of this conference, excessively general second-order questions about "science and religion" were not what we had in mind, could I nonetheless venture one brief remark of just that nature, about a certain asymmetry that needs to be taken into account between the two intellectual disciplines. It was Christian fundamentalists, largely originating in the United States in the late nineteenth century, who, duped by the impressive successes of natural science, felt elbowed out theologically thereby, and in so doing revealed in an explicit way what had been going on implicitly in their conception of theology, and more generally of Christian belief, namely that it was the sort of thing that could be edged out by natural science, or, more aggressively, could in its turn edge out natural science. That is to say, it became obvious that such Christian fundamentalists had all along implicitly supposed, and then in the late nineteenth century boldly and explicitly said, that science and religion are rivals, competing over common territory of explanation, as red and not-red compete over the common territory of the spectrum to their mutual exclusion. Terms not occupying common logical territory cannot stand in relations of mutual exclusion in the way that red and not-red do, and red and three o'clock in the afternoon don't and cannot: for three o'clock has no surface and red is timeless. And so we have today, in a late flourishing of that fundamentalist instinct, something or other of which, personally, I can make nothing, called "Creation science," standing, it is proposed, as red to contemporary cosmology's green. And as I have said, it is in the same way that we get a symmetrical parallel in the scientific fundamentalism of a Dawkins or a Dennett—of which, personally, I can make no better sense. I really have no historical explanation to offer of why these fundamentalisms flourished so vigorously in the mid- to late nineteenth century or why they do so more in dominantly Protestant intellectual cultures, like the United States or Britain, than they do in traditionally Catholic countries, like France, Spain, or Italy. Less still do I know why they have re-emerged with such renewed vigor in the early twenty-first century, and I will delay no longer on the issue, except to offer the following parable from my own field of medieval theology.

I think that we have seen all this before, and not alone in the sixteenth century, but also in the thirteenth. And we ought by now to be thoroughly sick of it. Instead I want to introduce to this conference the notion of the "demonstrable undecidable" as a category of propositions that occupies the space, or point of overlap or intersection (I still don't know which to call it), between the theologian and the cosmologist. Though it is not his terminology—I have borrowed it from the English philosopher Peter Geach—in his lifetime Thomas Aquinas got into serious trouble with some fairly unpleasant theological authorities in Paris and Oxford, and even with his genial and gentle friend and colleague in the University of Paris, Bonaventure, for employing this logical category in what his opponents thought was too loose a relation with Christian dogma. For Thomas argued that the question whether what exists, the universe, is of finite or of infinite duration is demonstrably undecidable, for rational argument can show that neither rational argument nor empirical evidence could settle the question one way or the other. In 1277, three years after his death, this opinion of Thomas's was formally condemned as heretical. Forty six years later Thomas was canonized and the condemnation revoked. Plus ça change. . . .

Mind you, the opposition was serious and heavyweight, because if on one side his Christian colleagues thought his position on the undecidability of the universe's duration was inconsistent with Christian faith, Thomas was opposed on the other side by one of his own preferred pagan authorities, Aristotle. For Aristotle thought that the eternity of the world was a rationally demonstrable truth, and in my view all parties, including today's cosmologists, ought to take Aristotle's argument seriously: for if invalid, it is interestingly rather than tediously so — as is the way with pretty much anything that Aristotle put his hand to. Faced with today's options, Aristotle would have said something like this: "Fine. You say that the universe's existence is of finite duration, and you gesture to an approximation of 13.7 billion years. But suppose today's cosmologist could achieve equivalently the sort of precision in dating the Big Bang that was achieved by an encyclopedia in my possession published in 1870, modestly entitled "Of All Human Knowledge," which seems to know that that universe was created at 11:00 a.m. on Thursday, October 24, 4004 BCE — then Aristotle would reply to today's cosmologists that they are just as misled as was my nineteenth-century encyclopedist. For if you suppose that time began at, say, 11:00 a.m. on October 24 13.7 billion years ago, then it follows that there cannot have been any countdown to the time when time began: it obviously cannot be the case that at 10:59 a.m. on that day there were sixty seconds to go before the clock started, and that for the obvious reason that there cannot have been a 10:59 a.m. on a day before there were any days or other times or time-measuring pieces of any kind. For of course Aristotle is right thus far: there is no "before" the beginning of time. Hence, he concludes,[5] there is no beginning to time. By the way, six centuries or more after Aristotle, Augustine thus far agreed: to ask what God was up to "then" before the beginning of time invites the response "Nothing at all," for the obvious reason that before the beginning of time there was no "then," hence no such "before."[6]

Thomas's response to Aristotle is the same as Augustine's to his interrogator: that he is simply muddled. Just because, manifestly, there can be no "before" the beginning of time — because time just is "the measure of change according to before and after" as Aristotle himself puts it — it does not follow that there was no beginning to time, and so no finite time-elapse since the clock began running. It does not follow, Thomas says, in agreement with his pious theological friends. Indeed, he says it is not true, because, along with those theological friends, he believed the book of Genesis tells us that time did have a beginning; but, in support of Aristotle, Thomas thinks that for all we would be in a position to say without the authority of scripture, it could have been true that the world is eternal, thus invoking the hostility of his pious theological enemies. In short, the duration of the universe's existence, all that there is other than God, is, for Thomas, demonstrably undecidable by any means other than our being informed on the matter by the Creator himself.

At this point, we really have upset the familiar apple carts. For not only does Thomas now have his favorite philosopher against him inasmuch as he rejects Aristotle's case that the world is provably eternal; in arguing that the universe's being eternal or not is either way indemonstrable he would now seem to have against him a holy alliance of you here at this conference, today's cosmologists worldwide, the philosophers, and along with them those conservative theologians of the thirteenth century. For both his thirteenth-century theological opponents and today's cosmologists maintain that the existence of the universe is demonstrably of finite duration, and, which is worse, the cosmologists of our times are able to calculate on the basis of empirical evidence pretty exactly how old it is. So it looks as if we can safely discount Thomas Aquinas if one is looking for theologians who can do some sort of better deal with the cosmologists than the fundamentalists of our times have on offer.

If that is the way it looks, then its looking that way shows you just how important it is to get some basic concepts clear before rushing to judgment. Above all it is important to get clear just what the cosmologists are claiming about what when they say that the universe is 13.7 billion years old. For are they not merely saying that as cosmologists what they are in a position to give an account of is 13.7 billion years old? I suppose there is no harm in calling what the cosmologist calculates to be 13.7 billion years old "the universe," even though there are string theorists who tell us that explaining the origin of fundamental physical laws in the observable universe requires the supposition that there are in addition to that which is 13.7 billion years old an indefinite number of other universes, the "multiverse," each existing within wholly different and unrelated time frames. So I repeat the question: Exactly what is the cosmologist saying is

13.7 billion years old? Everything? Anything? Or is it not rather just "this"? But if it is of just "this" that the cosmologist is asking the question "Why?" then I think Thomas is perfectly entitled to respond that the cosmologist could be right, and, for all he knows, is right: or perhaps he is entitled to say that necessarily what the cosmologist says is true, but trivially so, because the cosmologist's claim that the universe is 13.7 billion years old turns out to be nothing but the tautology that science can tell us the age of whatever phenomena science is equipped methodologically to tell the age of, and the demonstrative pronoun "this" simply points to what that is. That tells us nothing to counter Thomas's claim that the duration of there having been anything at all is empirically undecidable, just as it is rationally undecidable. Were it not that, as he thinks, the book of Genesis happens to tell us otherwise, for all we could know the world is eternal,[7] that is to say there being something or other in existence is of a duration without beginning and also, for all he knew (knowing nothing of entropy), of duration without end. And thus far we are left by Thomas with the disappointingly trivial conclusion that science can tell us whatever science can tell us, but whatever that is, it has no bearing on whether the world was created out of nothing. Nor, he adds, would it conflict with the proposition that the world was created out of nothing that its existence is of infinite duration, without beginning: for, as we might put it today, for all we know scientifically there might timelessly have been random fluctuations in a vacuum, and we would in that case be equally denied the right to say that such was the state of affairs before the Big Bang, if, that is, time comes into the picture only with the Big Bang. So, as Thomas says, it would be possible, if actually false, that there was no beginning to time. But in that case too the question "Why anything?" would still be intelligible, open, and in need of an answer about a universe endless in duration.

And so we generate the paradoxical conjunction of two propositions: first, that time is of finite extension, and second, that there is no "before" time's coming into existence. Hence, in a way it does not seem to make much difference whether you say, or whether you don't, that the Big Bang emerges out of random fluctuations in a vacuum ungoverned by temporal sequence and that time begins at a point calculated from the current state of the universe, its rate of expansion, and the length of time that, on the available observations, it must have taken for the universe to achieve that current state. The point is that there being, a fortiori, no antecedent temporal sequence "before" the emergence of time directly parallels the logic of the proposition that while the existence of anything at all needs accounting for, the description of the state of affairs "something or other exists" has no state of affairs with which to contrast, because since nothing is not a state of affairs, "out of nothing" is not a description of what anything's coming to exist is "out of." I have, of course, offered you no reasons for believing that the universe in truth is created. Nor will I. I am simply talking about what it would mean to say that the universe is created and about the logic that would govern any such claim.

The upshot is that we are left with the following picture. Science does what it does, and that's so much and no more. Theologians do what they do and it's not science. And therefore I don't mean that maintaining on biblical grounds that the universe is 4004 + 2011, that is, 6015, years old is wrong because it is bad science. I mean it is bad theology and isn't science at all, good or bad, it is *just* false, and anyway the Bible tells you nothing of the kind. In the meantime, as to the question whether what the scientist is accounting for by means of the Big Bang and what the Christian (or Jewish or Muslim) theologian refers to by the phrase "creation out of nothing" are one and the same event, differently described, I have nothing to say, not because I am peculiarly ignorant (though I am) but because the question is demonstrably undecidable. It is undecidable because even were they to want to, physicists could not get creation out of nothing to yield to scientific explanation, because scientific laws govern physical processes, and, as Thomas says, from "nothing" to "something" is not, and could not be, a describable law-governed trajectory; there is no such process. For from nothing to something is not a trajectory at all, or, as I have put it, at that point you aren't talking about any "from," you are denying there is one. But once you have a trajectory, there are laws governing it, and scientists can tell us what they are even back as far as to the singularity itself. And it really doesn't matter what those initial conditions are, they are something, and the question "Why?" can be asked of them: that is, the question can be asked, "How come there is *anything*?" no matter what. That gets a theologian and a philosopher going with something intelligible and rule governed to do. It's their day job. Of course, as a theologian I have no business expecting overtime rates for answers offered to the question "Why this?" Answering that is Priya's day job. But then in turn Priya has no business expecting double rates on any claim that her answer to the question "Why this?" *is* the answer to the question "Why anything?" It isn't. I just think we all have to get used to the idea that what the theologian and the cosmologist describe may be one and the same thing, for all we know. And we cannot know that they are, and we cannot know that they are not. But either way, the descriptions are not reducible to one another or to any common second-level master story, even if they do refer to one and the same thing. And that's as far as I can get with my bit of the story. Why anything, then? I haven't the first idea. But whatever it is that answers that question is what the name "God" names: not, then, any kind of supercause, just an unutterable mystery at the heart of whatever there is. And that, so far as I am concerned, will have to do for that.

EIGHT

The Price of Truth

Herbert McCabe on Love, Politics, and Death

"Nil hoc verbo veritatis verius" (Truth itself speaks truly, or there's nothing true). Thus, a trifle eccentrically, in the translation of Gerard Manley Hopkins, Thomas Aquinas's hymn *Adoro te devote*. I am greatly honored by the invitation to assist with the celebration here in Blackfriars Hall in Oxford of the eight-hundredth anniversary of the founding of the Order of Preachers, whose motto is *Veritas*, Truth. I am especially gratified to be doing so in this place named after that great sixteenth-century Dominican Bartolomé de las Casas, thoughts of whose commitment to the Dominican mission, at once intellectual and moral, caused me to reflect personally on what in my own experience of the Dominican order connects it distinctively with that motto. And right away one is caused to wonder why, of the two, the good and the true, the true is so often worsted in comparison with the good on a scale of warmth and energizing bite, reputed to be a cold, hard, static, and, as some will say, merely intellectual thing, less sensually motivating than the good. "'What is truth?' said jesting Pilate, though as Francis Bacon added, he didn't mean it and "would not stay for an answer." You can of course like Pilate be cynically and pessimistically postmodern about truth; I imagine, though, that a native Mayan in 1540 would not be inclined to see anything merely intellectual in the difference between a goody-two-shoes who supposes that the truth is something of interest only to people invested in what gets so easily dismissed these days as a hegemonic imperialistic culture and someone like Las Casas, for whom the truth was inseparable from "the way" and "the life" of a man who gets himself crucified for it all. And, these days, which fashionably dogmatic antiessentialist (they used to be called less approvingly "nominalists") truly wishes to deny Las Casas the one ground on which he could count in defense of the Maya people, namely that they were essentially human and could not be defined into enslavement in an abuse of power founded in an abuse of truth? For whom, then, is "the intellectual" something "mere"? Not, I think, for Dominicans. Less still for Mayans.

Within the contemporary English Dominican community committed to those intimate conjunctions between the truth, the way, and the life are many who have had and continue to have a transforming intellectual and moral influence on many of us. One of them, and here present, is a former master general of the order, Timothy Radcliffe, and Brian Davies over my way in Fordham is another, but I think also of that older generation of English and Scottish Dominicans that includes Laurence Bright, Simon Tugwell, Roger Ruston, Fergus Kerr, and, just so you know that I do not put all Dominicans together as if of a common theological mind, Thomas Gilby and Aidan Nicholls. Of course there was another of that company who embodied the distinctively Dominican commitment to the pursuit of truth—he was one of the greatest theologians of the English-speaking world in the late twentieth century—and you will know that I mean Herbert McCabe. Much influenced as he was by shifting combinations of influence of Ludwig Wittgenstein, Thomas Aquinas, and, on occasions, Karl Marx—I don't think he could always tell which of them caused what thoughts in his own mind—Herbert offered from that conjunction his distinctively practical take on "truth." To put it as simply as I can, if, for Herbert as for Christians commonly, the truth will set you free, also for him that same truth is likely to get you killed. In one of his more eccentric sermons (the one on the genealogy of Jesus as recounted in Matthew's gospel), having enumerated the succession of murderers, rapists, adulterers, tyrants, thieves, and prostitutes who together with a few more savory souls formed the ancestry of Jesus, Herbert remarks on how this shows that Jesus "belonged to us and came to help us, no wonder he came to a bad end, and gave us some hope."[1] The truth, death, and, connecting the two, love formed the core of Herbert's theology. It is some thoughts on his distinctive construal of their connections that I propose to offer you this evening.

HOT DOGS, COKE, AND THE EUCHARIST

It was in Dublin, and probably in 1966, that I first heard Herbert speak. Unsurprisingly, his topic was the Eucharist. Even in those good old days shortly after the end of the second Vatican Council, when more or less anything could get a run theologically, and did, Herbert was sometimes aggressively intolerant of loose theological talk. And when after his lecture he was asked by some common theologically liberal Catholic (of the sort Herbert could not abide) why it was that in that day and age we persisted in celebrating the Eucharist with the archaic elements of bread and wine, and whether a menu of, say, hot dogs and Coke would not be more meaningfully eucharistic in our times, Herbert replied in that nasal Northumbrian drawl of his, "I had always thought that the Eucharist had something to do with the meaning of food. Hot dogs and Coke, however, are without meaning. Anyway, they aren't food." Herbert often made you laugh. But witty as he was, he was rarely merely jocular, and his serious theological point went something like this.

Understanding the Eucharist requires an understanding of the meaning of food—giving life, sharing the gift, celebrating the giving, giving thanks in receiving, all wrapped up in the meaning of Jesus's death. Essentially, the Eucharist is a form of eating together, and its meaning is generated from an experiential basis in those social transactions that we call meals. No doubt meals vary in style from one culture to another. But hot dogs and Coke aren't a cultural variant. They are just universally deviant. That, of course, is the main reason why they won't do for the Eucharist. For, like them or not, hot dogs and Coke are fast food consumed on the trot, and corresponding with their calorific emptiness is their emptiness of human sociality. A fast-food joint is, indeed, full of sound and fury, but it signifies nothing. Hot dogs and Coke just don't make a human meal. So they can't make a eucharistic meal either.

But, Herbert went on, just as the Eucharist has to have some human meaning as food, so food is shown by the Eucharist to have a meaning that transcends the human. If no theology of the Eucharist can get going except on the basis of humanly meaningful practices of eating and drinking, the Eucharist shows those practices to be sacramental in that it reveals, and makes real, something divine about the meaning of eating and drinking of which otherwise we could not know. In short, through the Eucharist our human practices of eating and drinking are drawn into the eschatological mystery of the Trinitarian life itself, the bread and wine becoming the risen body of Christ, now in heaven: thereby eating is transformed, made new, made the Bread of Heaven. For the Eucharist shows how meals can take on a depth of meaning that altogether transcends, just as it depends upon, the human power to signify. And that again is why hot dogs and Coke won't do for a Eucharist. As food goes it is indeed fast. But as meaning goes, you would wait long for any hermeneutical, let alone any sacramental, depth.

Later on I will want to be a bit more explicit about how Herbert connected such considerations about the Eucharist with politics, but from the outset we ought to note that he would never have been satisfied with the notion that there is merely a parallel between that transforming, eschatological relation of Christianity to politics and the transforming, eschatological relation of the Eucharist to food. For just as the Eucharist is real food, so there is a certain sense in which through the Eucharist you can find a way into true politics. But before attempting to spell out how Herbert constructed this connection I should say a bit about some general propositions, epistemological and ethical, that he felt were presupposed to doing so.

The first of these is that while Herbert had much to say about the political he rarely seemed to have much to say in his writings about politicians or about what politicians think is the proper business of politics, which generally amounts, as I suppose he thought, to little more than politics in its hot-dogs-and-Coke manifestation. You have to see through the quotidian business of the politicians to something not less but more fundamentally political than they conceive of. That politicians are at the thin end of a wedge lacking in greater thickness at the other, that they believe what they do to be "real" politics, is, of course, one of the reasons why so many of them in Western democracies think of politics as their exclusive territory and believe that Christians, or religious people more generally, ought to stay in their place outside it. And it is also why so many right-wing Catholic Republicans in the United States appear to agree with them in rebuking Pope Francis for invading their territory of political issues, just as there are marginally left-of-center Democrats who rebuke him for invading their religion-free territory of personal morality. It's all the same either way.

For there would seem to be nothing much more than, as in a mirror, a mere horizontal reversal of the same elements in that reaction to the West's secularizing marginalization of the religious which causes some Christians to propose a reverse process of the resacralization of the political. The common element on both sides of this polarization is the notion that either way the political and the religious are construed as standing to one another as, so some say, do oil and water: they displace one another, and, unless they are methodologically constrained, they will inevitably invade one another's territories.

What is curious about this image of mutual exclusion, common to both the secularizers and the sacralizers, is that it is invoked on behalf of the distinctiveness of the religious and the political: they are "other" because they exclude one another. In fact, however, all that this metaphor of oil and water succeeds in doing is the opposite of that for which it is intended. For if you want to say that religion and politics are distinct, which you might well have good reasons for saying, you do need to mind your language and not cast that distinction in terms of mutual displacement, which, of course, is how oil and water stand to one another. And I think here we get to one of the major constructive features of Herbert's thought and writing, a key formal element making its presence felt in characteristic ways across his whole theology. It's an elementary bit of logic, but, as Peter Geach used to say, logic matters, and it has substantive consequences in ways often forgotten by, or else simply unknown to, politicians and theologians alike.

RELIGION, POLITICS, AND MUTUAL EXCLUSION

To keep things simple, two things can exclude one another only if they compete over the occupation of some common territory from which they *can* exclude one another—"red" and "green" exclude one another in the way that only colors can, whereas "red" and "six feet tall" do not and cannot exclude one another, because there is no common category from which one is excluded by the other's presence in it. Hence, given the conception of their difference as being one of mutual exclusion, if, as on the sacralization project, you wish to regain the territory of the religious on the political map—as some fundamentalist Christians in the United States still wish to do—it can only be at the cost of the autonomy of the political, which the politicians won't agree to. And if you wish to regain from the religious the territory of the political—as one might hope to do in Saudi Arabia—this can only be at the cost of the marginalization of the religious, which Saudi Arabians with equal ferocity resist. In respect of either dualism of the mutually exclusive, it was ever Herbert's inclination, at any rate negatively speaking, to visit a plague upon the houses of the secularizers and the sacralizers alike: for religion and politics are much more different than are oil and water, and for that reason they can be much more intimately related than either can envisage. And it is worth noting why this simple point in logic mattered so much to Herbert: to him it was foundational for the coherence of any possible Christian theology. You cannot, to take a central case, get the doctrine of the Incarnation right without it.

For if you want to say, as the ancient Council of Chalcedon bids us say, that one and the same person, Jesus Christ, was "wholly human and wholly divine," then it is essential that you have ways of saying and showing that the utter transcendence of the uncreated Godhead cannot entail the exclusion of the full humanity of Christ, nor the other way round. On the contrary, Chalcedon's Christology is the language of intimacy, not of exclusion. For which reason if it is not to be self-contradictory to speak of the Incarnation as Chalcedon does, then the one relation in which the divine and the human cannot stand is that between oil and water. For that is straightforward Nestorianism, when it isn't its contrary opposite, Sabellianism, and either Jesus's humanity will be affirmed only in denial of the divinity or the divinity is affirmed at the cost of the human.

Then there is a second group of preliminaries with which we need to engage if we are to get Herbert's eucharistic parallel right, and first of all a couple of philosophical remarks. For Herbert, as I said, the Eucharist deepens the meaning of food. It reveals something unexpected in the human meanings we achieve by eating and drinking together, of which, without the Eucharist, we could know nothing. And so what he had in mind to say about the relation of the Eucharist to food is this: you do not fully understand the human meaning of food until you understand its eucharistic depth. Lurking within the quotidian business of eating meals together is a mysterious dimension, waiting to be disclosed. And then, chasing the parallel through, Herbert would add that you do not fully understand the human meaning of the political until you understand its theological depth.

In affirming that the Eucharist deepens the human meaning of eating and drinking, Herbert had something in mind to deny, namely that the Eucharist simply adds, as it were superveniently, a further theological meaning to the human meaning of food, such that you might, if you have faith, prefer to see food that way—rather as one might happen to see (as synesthetically I do) Thursday as a yellow day of the week and Tuesday as blue. That, roughly, is the Lutheran account of the real presence of Christ in the Eucharist: it was what Luther called "companation," the simultaneous coexistence of bread and wine and the body and blood of Christ as parallel realities. The Eucharist is not the presence of Christ as an add-on meaning of eating and drinking together: it *is* the meaning of eating and drinking together. It's just that you need faith to see through to the depths of that human meaning, depths that we know of as the Incarnation, which shows us that the truly human is always beyond the grasp of the merely human; or, as we say, the bread and wine are shown truly to have become the body and blood of Christ—and only now do we understand their meaning.

WHOSE REALITY?

As I say, there is an issue of philosophical importance lying behind these truth claims of faith, an issue at once about meaning and about what there is, an issue of ontology, as we say. The Eucharist tells us something about real food, about what food is really like—as distinct from its fantastical fast forms. Now, for too long our everyday perceptions of what is real have been weighed down under the pressure of empiricist philosophies, which, to put it in a rather casual metaphor, would have us construe the real as what we bump into, the hard knocks, as it were, of immediate experience, and that, by contrast, meanings are mediated, secondary, and soft derivations from those hard knocks, standing at a greater or lesser distance from the real. The real, on this account, is the immediate. But this empiricist prioritization of experience's directness over the supposedly indirect and mediated character of meaning gets everything the wrong way round for the purposes of understanding Herbert's theology.

One way into what is at issue here is through the notion of "abstraction," the old-fashioned word of early modern School philosophy, used to describe the mental process by which meaning is grasped. The trouble with this word is that in today's philosophical vocabularies it seems to suggest—and it has done so since at least John Locke in the late seventeenth century—a process of thinning concepts out to the degree of common meaning that all and only their individual instances possess: and that can be little enough. "Featherless biped" after all, is a description that will identify everything that is a human being and nothing that isn't, but the phrase hardly invites you into the rich experience of members of our species. Concepts, or "ideas," as Locke calls them, are, in his sense of the word, "abstractions," essentially simplifications, minimal paraphrases of complex objects of experience.

Thomas Aquinas's account of abstraction reverses all this. If you bump into three hard objects in a darkened room, you are in possession of Lockean purely abstract impressions of them, that is to say, you have grasped of all three objects that they possess in common the property of solidity, discounting any other properties that in the dark are invisible. If, however, you then turn on a light, you see them all in the medium of much greater complexity and variety: you experience them no longer minimally as tangible objects, but in their complexity as furniture. You grasp their wealth of differentiation in respect of position and color and shape and size and elegance—or for that matter ugliness if ugly they are—their usefulness, their layout; you begin to understand the social places and purposes of the room thus furnished. It's now seen to be a sitting room. And as you learn more and more about what you see, you more and more successfully grasp the meaning of the sensory inputs, precisely in your grasp of their complex variety, their diversity and differentiation. And so it is that you know what kind of room you are in, you know where you are, and the experience is now intelligible, as Thomas would say. So he says that the mind's forming concepts out of particular experiences is like turning on a light: it reveals the color of those experiences, it thickens them up, reveals their depths and densities. It does not, as Locke thought, thin experience out. Lockean abstractions are passive, pale, and effete; they are, as Hume was later to say of what he calls "ideas," faded sense impressions. Thomas's abstractions are, on the contrary, polychrome; they are dense and saturated powers of judgment about the world.

And when Wittgenstein sought an account of how meaning is grasped, having little taste for the Lockean language of abstraction, he thought of it as more like learning how to use a vocabulary, a lexicon, or, as he called it, a language game: you get some way toward knowing what "human" means to the degree that you have mastered the use of a hugely complex and varied discourse, not by a sort of intellectual staring at a single concept, for such mastery is shown by way of a capacity to generate ever more varied, complex, and refined judgments. Of course, Wittgenstein was right to abandon the old Schoolman's word *abstraction* in view of its having been taken over by that common Lockean meaning, for in Locke's sense it has passed over into ordinary usage to such an extent that it is unusable today; and certainly in today's usage it offers nothing in respect of Thomas's account of judgment formation. In any case, on the account of meaning that you find all over Herbert's work, we get at the meaning of a complex nature as Thomas and Wittgenstein thought of it when we grasp not some abstract idea but, on the contrary, the complex differentiations of the concrete, the living reality of a segment of the world, how that reality signifies for a linguistic community; and so it is that thereby you come to understand what languages you need to learn in order to experience the world with any degree of adequacy to its complexity. And if concepts were for Thomas in this way polychrome, for Wittgenstein they are polyglot: they speak in many tongues all at once. For Thomas and Wittgenstein, by way of what the Schoolmen once meant by abstraction you get nearer to, not further away from, the reality of a thing than any sense experience can get. By abstraction you get at once to the complexity of a thing's relationships, its essence, and its depths.

When therefore Herbert said that the Eucharist reveals a depth within the human transactions of eating and drinking, he meant what Thomas meant when he said that understanding the concept of something is like throwing a light on it, revealing it in its full, concrete variety and differentiation: the Eucharist shows us something in the meaning of eating that otherwise we could not see. It does not superveniently add on an optional extra.[2] And, to speak in very general terms, Herbert's disdain for our quotidian conception of politics amounts to this equivalently: in truth it is the politicians' and the political commentators' conception of the political that is a Lockean abstraction, for in our day-to-day political practices the politicians are like nothing so much as persons bumping into hard, massy, objects in the dark: as they crack their shins they protest that that is all there is to be experienced in the real world of politics. Naturally they will suppose that the theologians have nothing to say if they know nothing of their bruises. Therefore, as I should say by contrast, in how he envisaged its standing to the political the Eucharist was, for Herbert, like turning on a light: other realities, other depths, of the political are shown forth, because there is more there than is known in the politicians' abstract experiences, and the Eucharist reveals that more. In turning away from the politicians Herbert was far from turning away from politics. He was telling you what real politics is. The meaning of the political is to be found in the meaning of the Eucharist.

PROPAGANDA, IDEOLOGY, AND SIN

Next, a contrasting word, about politics and sin, about sin as politics—not, you will be glad to hear, about the sins of politicians, interestingly scarlet as often they are; nor particularly about your sins and mine, most of which are uninteresting and merely gray; but about sin as it is understood in the expression "the sin of the world," to which Herbert frequently adverted as one of several key themes that he had found in the gospel of John. It is, he noted, as having taken away the sin of the world that John the Baptist first introduces Jesus to his own followers (John 1:29), and whatever he meant by Jesus's having "taken [it] away," by "the sin of the world" Herbert took the author of the fourth gospel not to be referring to anyone's individual sins, howsoever interestingly scarlet. He referred rather to a rather tediously common sinful predicament, to the primordial mess that we are all collectively in willy-nilly, rather than to the mess that we personally make of things, and therefore to a general condition of sinfulness that in one way or another mediates all our actions, whether personally sinful or innocent. The world, Christians say, is a fallen world. In fact, Herbert seems right here: the author of John's frequent references to "the world"—as when Jesus says in his last discourse that the world will hate you[3]—simply refers to the pervasively fallen condition of things. There is a world of sin, sin has made a universe for itself. And one of the consequences of the world's sinfulness is that the world does not know things, does not see things that are there to be seen: it does not know the truth, its own truth. The fallen world is bumping around in the dark and is much bruised in consequence. And politics of the hot dogs and Coke variety, like everything else, is firmly set within that world.

It may be guessed from these last remarks, and if so, then correctly, that Herbert's principal interest in attempting to explicate this notion of the world's sin is with epistemology, with the way in which our fallen human condition shows up in failures of human perception, of seeing and of knowing, with how our being fallen is a general condition on social cognition: the world falsifies; that is what it does, the world in this Johannine sense is the reason why we do not know the truth. And here it is unsurprising if Herbert, particularly in his writing in the sixties and seventies, called upon Marx for an explanation. For as to its effects on how we humans perceive our social world, the sin of the world is productive of what, from Marx, he learned to call "ideology."

IDEOLOGY AND PROPAGANDA

By *ideology* Marx does not refer to the routine practices of lies and propaganda, that is to say, to the corrupt activity engaged in by interest groups, whether in possession of or seeking to acquire political or economic power, conscious devices of social communication designed to skew a people's perceptions of political reality by rhetorical or coercive means. By *ideology* you do not mean what Fox News in the United States or in the United Kingdom the *Daily Mail* contribute to the news, deliberate falsifications, failures of truthfulness, that you can check out simply by consulting the facts. By *ideology* Marx meant a "society's natural and spontaneous mode of thought."[4] Ideology is a more complex socially cognitive formation than propaganda. Propaganda has an author. The propagandist seeks to impose refutable untruths or distortions by the use of force, or charm, or seduction, or hook, crook, bribery, or simple cover-up, but in any case tactically, because someone, or some agency, is somewhere actively lying or otherwise deliberately skewing the facts. Ideologies, by contrast, arise endogenously out of the very meaning of the social relations we transact; they are the social world as we consistently and as a matter of course misperceive it because the social relations themselves that govern our interactions with one another are constructed out of those misperceptions. If ideology is illusion, it is illusion embedded in routine social practices; ideology is a society's common sense, its lived "matter of course," even if, as G. K. Chesterton observed (I think in *Orthodoxy*) much common sense is, as a matter of course, uncommon nonsense.

Now just as in this way ideologies are natural, spontaneous, and internal to the social practices they arise from, so are the structures of misperception of a fallen world. I think Herbert thought of sin mainly in these terms, as socially structured misperception, as human beings systematically relating amiss, misperceiving the truth of themselves and living out "really" those misperceptions. A fallen world does not know its own truth; above all it must misrecognize its own condition as fallen. It lives falsely and falsifies life.

THE SIN OF THE WORLD

It follows that there is an important distinction between the cognitive dissonances of an ideology and those of that general condition that John refers to as the world's sin, even if they occur upon a continuous line of deceptions. For an ideology will be one historically specific form in which the sin of the world appears. In theory we can construct particular causal explanations of an ideology, we can after all analyze out that diffuse and pervasive system of embedded economic practices, perceptions, and value judgments that we call the market, "spontaneous and natural" modes of thought though they be. We can diagnose them, we can account for their historical occurrence, and we could hope critically to engage with them from within some ground of perception and thought free of that ideology—such as Marxism itself. And Herbert thought Marx must be right about that, at least as a minimum necessary condition of critical moral and social thought, even if he never supposed Marx provided their sufficient conditions. For Herbert thought that all social critique ought to begin from Marx, even if, as we will see, he also thought that the demands of the truth required more than Marx could offer, a truth that in fact Marx set about systematically denying.

For what John in his gospel calls the "sin of the world" is a condition that is too universal to be laid at the door of any particular cause, for everything whatever is subject to its conditioning, including Marxism. I suppose that this is what Calvin meant when he spoke of our fallen condition as one of a depravity that is "total," for everything whatever is depraved by it, even if not totally: even the very instruments of social and political criticism are themselves blunted and infected thereby. We cannot get behind the falsifications to some standing ground that is in principle unfalsifiable and ideology-free. Unsurprisingly, then, there is no proper causal account in adequately theoretical terms of human fallenness, but only images and foundational narratives. And that is why even the best known of these narratives of sin's origins, those of Genesis, do no more than disguise, without resolving, the contradiction they embody. The story Genesis tells doesn't work as it stands, as most exegetes of it from Origen in the second century to our times know: for how can Adam and Eve succumb to the temptation to seek the "knowledge of good and evil" unless they are already in possession of that knowledge as a condition of their being tempted in the first place, never mind of their yielding to it? The lesson of Genesis is clear: there can be no etiology of the sin of the world, since any explanation of its origin must presuppose that fallenness as its causal condition.

I think it was his insistence upon this completely general character of sin, of its being the general condition of a fallen world, that differentiated

Herbert's response to the political from that of his third major source of inspiration, after Thomas and Wittgenstein, in Marx. The political critique of a fallen world is bound to be distinct from the political critique of a historically particular political formation, even though in either case these formations share the general character of being structured upon systems of misperception of their own reality. Contrary to some misreadings of Herbert's position, he never identified the "world" of John's gospel with capitalism, even if he took it for granted that capitalism was its late modern instantiation. However could he, since he was convinced of the relevance of history, and the emergence of mercantilist-capitalist economies in twelfth-century Italy is hardly what the author of the fourth gospel had in mind? And Herbert certainly maintained that even though there can be no moral equivalence between capitalism and the socialist critique of it, nonetheless socialism was subject to the same conditions of fallenness as are exhibited by the capitalism it critiques. The world cannot know itself on its own terms: its socially organized structure of internally generated misperception is pervasive, universal. That is to say, because of the way the world is, its sin not only causes misperception of the fallen world in general but recursively generates the misperception of the sin that causes it to be fallen. As it were, sin cannot truthfully tell its own story; it has no power of its own to know the truth of itself: sin tells lies even about sin. And what Herbert was ever after was an answer to the question: What narrative tells the true story of sin? Which one of us is in a position to tell that story of sin who is not also complicit in the sin the story tells of? How can we know the truth of ourselves in practice? For Herbert the answer to all those questions has to be the same: the death of Jesus on the cross is what finally reveals the world's sin to itself. Confronted by a wholly human human being, a being whose reality as human is too much for a fallen humankind to bear, the world has nothing to offer of its own except to kill him.

So it is just here that we get to the heart of Herbert's theology. There was only one issue for him, and that had to do with how to love in a world whose characteristic and sustaining practices showed it to be the political routinization of sin and so of the rejection of love. And Herbert's answer, from the time of that lecture in Dublin in 1965 to the day he died in 2001, was always to my knowledge the same: it takes an innocent man's being killed finally to expose and resolve the conflict between love and the world, not because there was no alternative available to God, for, as Thomas says, the slightest twitch of the divine finger would have done it, a nod and a wink, but just because the true nature of God would be revealed only by a solution so radical that it is at once wholly surprising and wholly right, at once supererogatory and "just so." For, as Thomas says, "God's generosity is uniquely and wholly over the top" ("Ipse solus est maxime liberalis" is the Latin): for God "does nothing simply for his own benefit, everything as an expression of sheer goodness."[5]

"CHRISTIAN POLITICS" AND THE MARTYR'S DEATH

Everything for Herbert followed from that. It was from there that he began to talk about revolution, that acknowledgment of the surplus demand that at once is generated by the given fact and exceeds its capacity to meet. Revolution is nothing but the supererogatory as political practice. Always you heard Herbert say, the revolution that a Christian politics calls for is nothing so limited as a revolution in society: it is nothing so limited as that, because no revolution in society could be final that is not also a revolution in the body itself, achieved in its death and resurrection. As Paul said, the final enemy, the ultimate limitation imposed upon all human agency, and so on the political, is imposed not by sin, but by sin's consequence, which is death. Hence the only revolutionary hope that is not groundlessly utopian lies in the transformation of what Paul calls the "body of death" itself; it lies in the resurrection.

Necessarily, then, the Christian orientation to the political is from the edge, the edge represented by the acceptance of death as the price of love. Herbert would say that the world is so desperately in need of its false consciousness that it will kill rather than have it exposed in its true colors as the refusal of unconditioned love that it is. That is why Christians cannot construct their politics from the center ground. This is not because its claims are marginal. Christianity views the political from the margin because the center ground of politics is dominated by a practical untruth, an ideological misrecognition of its own nature and conditionality— because, to repeat, the world's sin is such that it cannot know its own truth, not even politically. Otherwise put, the politics of a sinful world inverts everything. It has centered the marginal and has marginalized its own center. And the church, therefore, stands centered upon what the sin of the world has pushed out to the margin. The church is a sort of disloyal opposition. It's not that it takes the other side on a shared agenda. It's more like the reply the man in Galway gave when asked how to get from there to Limerick: "If I were you I wouldn't start from here."

It is for this reason that Christian faith cannot be translated out directly into any political program without being subjected to a reductive secularization. In short, the world's truth can exist only in an unresolvable tension with the world whose truth it is, a tension unresolvable until the sin of the world and its condition of mortality are finally overcome. But does all this entail that there is in the meantime no Christian political praxis? And if indeed there is, how did Herbert envisage it?

Herbert was a socialist and at least a Marxist, if a lot more besides, and could not imagine how a Christian who read the gospels could consistently be anything else. But socialism too has its hot-dogs-and-Coke variety of politics and as such could never get to the point, because you had got to the point only when you had confronted in the last resort nothing so trivial as a trump in the Donald version, but all such politics as his that represents the politics of death, for it is death itself that is swept away in the Last Trump of All, the *last* enemy. For Herbert, revolution was simply the Resurrection—the triumph of the body over death—as politics. Consequently, for Herbert, there is of course a Christian political praxis—if that is what you wish to call it, though it might be better just to call it a foregone conclusion. It consists in the price that is to be paid for our resurrection and therefore is exhibited in a spectacular way in the lives, but more than in their lives, in the foregone conclusion of their deaths, of Oscar Romero and of Martin Luther King, of Mahatma Gandhi, of Dietrich Bonhoeffer, of the five women martyrs of El Salvador, and of countless other martyrs who threatened the world's powers with the exposure of their own truth, the truth that the world must keep itself from knowing.

Those martyrs knew that they were challenging the world, that they were pushing it to its last resort to own the truth that it had willfully marginalized, knowing that as a last resort it would kill to ensure that it was not revealed for what it is. For at all costs the world needs not to know its own truth, since its power depends on an ignorance that, once exposed, is willful. And so, as one theologically minded worldly power very sensibly observed, "It is expedient that one man should die for the sake of the people," though somehow it always seems to turn out that there is just one more death-dealing strategy that is expedient for the people's sake. Those deaths are paradigmatic for a Christian politics, whose nature is essentially that of the prophet, of the seer. For what the world needs to do in order to suppress the knowledge of its own truth is precisely what reveals its lie: its need to kill. Correspondingly, the martyr is no innocent but passive, accidental victim of the crush of circumstance, nor any merely Promethean hero. Martyrs are those who have willingly placed themselves in the way of that collision, embracing death as love's price, because they stand exactly at the point of eschatological intersection between love and death that Herbert identified as the church's position of critical marginality, the most telling quotidian theological expression of which was of course for him the Eucharist.

Those deaths, then, are prophetic indeed. But there is no need to overdramatize this conclusion, neither did Herbert ever do so. For to stand at that point of eschatological collision is the ordinary condition of the Christian—it was of course where Bartolomé de Las Casas stood—and of this ordinary condition the martyr is but the exceptional, hyperbolic, instance. So the ordinary practice of the Christian, of the church, is the Eucharist, the celebration of a martyr's death, as it were, getting the martyr's death into our bones. Therein is a kind of disambiguation, a final clearing away of the fog of all ideology. The praxis of the Christian reveals the world for what it is, revealing what on its own terms it needs to be—it needs its last resort of violence. For the world feeds on death.

The death of martyrs is therefore paradigmatic for a Christian politics: martyrdom is the church's principle of verification. It is not that there is no quotidian form of Christian intervention in the political, though what form and shape in detail such intervention may take is a story for another theologian—it was never Herbert's primary concern. But if for another theologian, it is not another story. For martyrdom remains the eschatological paradigm for all Christian political action, the paradigm of its praxes. Those martyrs' deaths tell you something that no Christian political program could otherwise tell you. They do not tell you what to do. They tell you no more than where to stand, that is, where Las Casas stood.

They tell you what you will see when you stand there, for it is only when you stand there that the truth can appear over the horizon. And they tell you that, standing there, you will discover the price of the truth that you see. For one way or another, the world will cut you down where you stand.

This, then, is the supererogatory practice of the Christian, the above and beyond that is Christianity's default. Herbert, as ever, put it most memorably in perhaps his best-known *obiter*. "If you do not love," he used to say, "you are dead. But if you do love, you will be killed."

NOTES

ONE. How Could a Good God Allow Evil?

1. David Hume, *Dialogues Concerning Natural Religion* 10, ed. Martin Bell (Harmondsworth: Penguin Books, 1990), 108–9.

2. See Brian Davies, *Thomas Aquinas on God and Evil* (Oxford: Oxford University Press, 2011); David Burrell, *Deconstructing Theodicy: Why Job has Nothing to Say to the Puzzle of Suffering* (Brazos Press: Grand Rapids, MI, 2008); and also Herbert McCabe, *God and Evil in the Theology of Thomas Aquinas*, ed. Brian Davies (New York: Continuum, 2010).

3. My wife Courtney Palmbush vigorously contests my insensitivity here.

4. Perhaps. Perhaps not if it is good for the species that lambs are culled, and maybe better if this is done by lions and other natural predators rather than by human beings herding them into ghastly slaughterhouses.

5. "Tyger, tyger burning bright." Courtney Palmbush reminds me that for Blake the consistency of a creation containing herbivorous lambs together with lamb-eating tigers is a problem. I agree that it is a problem for lambs. But I cannot see that it is a problem about God.

6. Hume, *Dialogues Concerning Natural Religion* 2.6, ed. Bell, 81.

7. Hume, *Dialogues Concerning Natural Religion* 9, ed. Bell, 116.

8. It seems to be thought by some that we have the universe we have not because it is the only universe actual and was created such but because there is an indefinite number of possible worlds, every one of which is actual and so, necessarily, is ours. There is less reason to believe this hypothesis than that this world was created by God: at least the belief in a creator God is in principle defeasible (as such atheists also propose to show by the existence of evil). That every possible universe exists is, by contrast, a shameless piece of unfalsifiable metaphysics, devised, it would seem, merely for the purposes of seeing God out of the picture.

9. Julian of Norwich, *A Revelation of Love*, in *The Writings of Julian of Norwich*, ed. Nicholas Watson and Jacqueline Jenkins (University Park: Pennsylvania State University Press, 2006), 121–381.

10. It is extraordinary how naive some atheistic apologists have become about this, somehow persuading themselves (but hardly any one else) that our times are

morally superior to all others, this improvement being down to the decline of religious belief. It is hard to believe that our times are morally superior all round, plausible to believe that they are morally superior in some ways, and wholly silly to have to think of them as morally superior on account of the waxing of secularization and the waning of religious belief. Such a view seems to consist in nothing but the transaction of one degree of wishful thinking for another, dogma for dogma.

11. Julian of Norwich, *Revelation of Love*, chap. 27.

12. There is here what philosophers call an "omega inconsistency": the proposition "Necessarily there are some evil actions" does not entail of any evil action whatever that it was necessary.

13. Strictly speaking this is a non sequitur. God could of course create that world in which, as it happens, no one actually freely sins. What on Plantinga's account God cannot do is create a world such that no one freely sins.

14. Julian of Norwich, *Revelation of Love*, chap. 27.

15. Though this particular formula is found only in her subsequently revised and much expanded Short Text, chap. 10; it looks as if Julian expunged that particular way of putting it in the Long Text, written perhaps thirty years later, for the very good reason that it seemed to set the divine and human agencies in opposition to one another in exactly the way that she rejects in the Long Text.

16. Moreover, "best possible" is ambiguous here between (a) a Platonic notion of the ideal form of the string quartet, which, as Plato saw it, could not be an individual instance of the string quartet and could not therefore be actually composed, and (b) the best string quartet that could actually be composed. Unhappily, there do not seem to be any criteria for determining of any actual string quartet that there could not be a better one. These seem to be the options, and neither seems to make sense of the description "best possible string quartet."

17. Of course it isn't: one fewer victim of the Holocaust would have been better than the historical total, and perfectly possible.

18. Proverbs 8:31.

19. And if you are still unhappy with this view of Mozart, then substitute Haydn, who is the supreme master of unpredicted but retrodictable surprises.

20. This way of putting the matter will perhaps arouse hostility from some biblical theologians and scholars of our times (their hackles tend to rise at the least provocation) as entailing or embodying a form of supercessionism. This is the theology that denies of the Hebrew scriptures any autonomous meaning of its own and allows only such meaning as consists in their fulfillment in the Christian scriptures. There is need to set these two levels of meaning in conflict with one another only on very odd assumptions about scriptural literalness that disallow two-way hermeneutical transactions between the Hebrew and Christian scriptural texts.

21. Julian of Norwich, *Revelation of Love*, chap. 27.

22. Alvin Plantinga, *The Nature of Necessity* (Oxford: Clarendon, 1974), 186.

23. J. L. Mackie, "Evil and Omnipotence," *Mind* 64, no. 254 (1955): 209.

24. Julian of Norwich, *Revelation of Love,* chap. 27, 79.
25. Julian of Norwich, *Revelation of Love,* chap. 86, 379.
26. John Milton, *Paradise Lost,* preface.
27. Julian of Norwich, *Revelation of Love,* chap. 32.

T W O. "One with God as to the Unknown"

1. "Per revelationem gratiae in hac vita non cognoscamus de Deo quid est, et sic ei quasi ignoto coniungamur." Thomas Aquinas, *Summa theologiae* (hereafter *ST*) 1a, q. 12, art. 13, ad. 1.

2. In this Thomas Aquinas and Duns Scotus disagree, Scotus maintaining that the natural object of the human mind is the thisness of the things that it knows, their individuation, Thomas thinking that we can know individuals only in the medium of the kinds they instantiate.

3. Sermon 83, "Renovamini Spiritu," in Meister Eckhart, *The Essential Sermons, Commentaries, Treatises and Defense,* ed. and trans. Edmund College, O. S. A., and Bernard McGinn (London: SPCK, 1981), 208.

4. *ST* 1a, q. 3, prol.

5. *ST* 1a, q. 2, art. 3.

6. For a translation of a fragment of Giles's commentary on the Song of Songs, see my *Eros and Allegory* (Kalamazoo, MI: Cistercian Publications, 1995), 363.

7. I might emphasize *medieval* nun. Teresa of Avila in the early modern period complains of how she was as a woman forbidden the reading of the Song of Songs except for brief citations in the Office for the Feast of the Assumption of the Virgin Mary; see her *Meditations on the Song of Songs* 6.8, in *The Collected Works of Teresa of Avila,* trans. Kieran Kavanagh and Otilio Rodriguez (Washington, DC: Institute of Carmelite Studies, 1980), 2:253. There were no such prohibitions in the Middle Ages, nuns taking up the full text with enthusiasm.

8. Though his colleague and friend at the University of Paris, St. Bonaventure, does it in his own way in his monograph the *Itinerarium mentis in Deum,* which maps the theological progress of study in the academy directly onto the "journey of the soul into God."

9. On this, see especially Simon Tugwell's essay, "Prayer, Humpty-Dumpty and Thomas Aquinas," in *Language, Meaning and God, Essays in Honour of Herbert McCabe OP,* ed. Brian Davies, O.P. (London: Geoffrey Chapman, 1987), 24–50.

10. *ST* 3a, q. 21, art. 4, corp. One might fairly translate a little more forcefully so as to let Thomas's meaning get through: "We need to pray if we are to get to know what are our true desires."

11. *ST* 3a, q. 21, art. 2, corp.

12. See Oscar Cullmann, *Immortality of the Soul or Resurrection of the Dead: The Witness of the New Testament* (London: Epworth, 1964).

13. *ST* 3a, q. 21, art. 4, ad. 1.
14. *ST* 3a, q. 21, art. 2, corp.
15. Isaiah 53:3.

THREE.   Reason, the Eucharist, and the Body

In the first draft of this paper (of which this is a revision) I was much indebted to four former graduate students in the Faculty of Divinity in Cambridge (as they were then some fifteen years ago) for their careful, perceptive, and helpful comments: Férdia Stone-Davis, Vittorio Montemaggi, Donna Lazenby and Ed Morgan. For this much-corrected version I am equally indebted to Fergus Kerr for pointing out an important error of historical judgment contained in that earlier version.

1. Denys Turner, *Faith, Reason, and the Existence of God* (Cambridge: Cambridge University Press, 2014), 3–6.

2. *Dogmatic Constitution on the Catholic Faith*, in *Decrees of the Ecumenical Councils*, ed. Norman Tanner, S.J., vol. 2, *Trent to Vatican II*, 810.

3. See Thomas Aquinas, *Summa theologiae* [hereafter *ST*] 1a, q. 1, art. 1, corp.

4. Fergus Kerr, "Knowing God by Reason Alone: What Vatican I Never Said," *New Blackfriars* 91 (2010): 215–28.

5. In *ST* 1a, q. 2, art. 1, Thomas asks whether God's existence is "*demonstrabile.*" He answers that it is. In q. 2, art. 3, he asks whether there is a God, and he answers that there is, and that God's existence "*probari potest.*" It is difficult not to conclude that if in other contexts the connections are sometimes looser, here for Thomas *demonstrare* and *probare* make identical demands of conclusiveness: you get *demonstratio* only where you have *probatio*, and you have *probatio* only where you have argument that is formally valid as to inference and sound as to the truth of the premises.

6. Thomas Aquinas, *Peri hermeneias* 6.17a.33–35.

7. Indeed probably a majority of scholars think that even Thomas doesn't agree with this account, believing that, for him, reason gets to work on God only within a faith that presupposes God's existence. I leave that issue aside here, since I am confident still in the case against that reading of Thomas that I presented in *Faith, Reason, and the Existence of God* back in 2004.

8. Fergus Kerr, *After Aquinas: Versions of Thomism* (Oxford: Blackwell, 2002), 67.

9. J. J. C. Smart and John J. Haldane, *Atheism and Theism* (Oxford: Blackwell, 1996), 143.

10. *ST* 1a, q. 16, art. 8, ad. 4.

11. I am grateful to Donna Lazenby for putting it this way.

12. Actually his point only really works in French: "Tout autre est tout autre," he says, either is a tautology ("Every other is every other") or else means that there is only complete otherness, so that God is not the only completely other, because all othernesses are as complete as God's, it's all the same as othernesses go. Extraordinary. The study of philosophy endlessly exceeds one's expectations of it, in this case of just how wrong philosophers can get it.

13. *ST* 1a, q. 1, art. 8.

14. See chapter 8 below, the section "Whose Reality?," for further discussion of this maximalist conception of reason and of its theological deployment.

15. Thomas does not suppose that our being animals is part of what we humans are. It is the whole of what we humans are, our difference from the brute animals being included "indeterminately" in our generic animality. We are, therefore, wholly animals of a certain kind: "Quicquid est in specie, est etiam in genere ut non determinatum. Si enim animal non esset totum quod est homo, sed pars eius, non praedicaretur de eo, cum nulla pars integralis de suo toto praedicetur." (Whatever falls within the species also falls indeterminately within the genus. For if being an animal were not the whole of what a man is, but only a part, it would not be predicable of a man, since no integral part is predicated of the whole.) *De ente et essentia,* chap. 2. See chapter 2 of my *Thomas Aquinas, a Profile* (New Haven, CT: Yale University Press, 2014).

16. For more on this, see my *Thomas Aquinas,* chaps. 2 and 3.

17. Dante, *De vulgari eloquentia* 1.2, ed. and trans. Steven Botterill (Cambridge: Cambridge University Press, 1999), 5–7.

18. Thomas does not suppose that our being rational is but a part of what we humans are. It is the whole of what we are as being just that kind of animal. Hence, insofar as our being animals implies that we have bodies, our being rational implies that we have bodies that are included within our natures as rational: "Sic ergo genus significat indeterminate totum id quod est in specie, non enim significat tantum materiam; similiter etiam differentia significat totum et non significat tantum formam." (For this reason the genus ["animal"] indeterminately signifies all that falls within the species, it does not signify the matter only; in the same way the difference ["rational"] signifies the whole and not only the form.) *De ente et essentia,* chap. 2.

19. I am much indebted in what follows to Vittorio Montemaggi for many informative conversations on the subject of Dante, meaning, and the body.

20. Just as, under other conditions (such as my mentioning the example above), it is an instruction on how to promise, e.g., you are going to need the form of words "I promise" or some such; such instructions are not themselves promises made.

21. Herbert McCabe, "The Eucharist as Language," in *Catholicism and Catholicity, Eucharistic Communities in Historical and Contemporary Perspectives,* ed. Sarah Beckwith (Oxford: Blackwell, 1999), 26.

22. Just as the italicizations in this sentence do visually.

23. Oliver Davies, *Meister Eckhart, Mystical Theologian* (London: SPCK, 1991), 180.

24. McCabe, "Eucharist as Language," 26. Dale Martin, of the Department of Religious Studies at Yale, objected when I read this paper there that what I say hereafter about music is too "essentialist," as if to say there is just some one set of characteristics possessed of all music in all times and cultures, which he doubted. It is true that what I say about music here is based upon reflection on a certain classical paradigm in the Western tradition, perhaps, say, the late string quartets of Beethoven or Schubert; and possibly my account of music would not be true of other times, cultures, and traditions. I do not for my part know. In any case I am happy to allow a mental reservation on the part of any reader who doubts the universal applicability of what I say about music here: it will make no difference at all to my argument if anyone prefers to do so.

25. Though she should not be held responsible for what I have drawn from them here, the following remarks about music and language owe much to discussions with Férdia Stone-Davis, as also to her unpublished paper "Plato, Kant and the Reduction of Music," delivered to the Music Research Group conference "The Intellectual Frontiers of Music" at the University of Aberdeen, June, 2002.

26. In Leuven I once attended a recital of the stanzaic poetry of Hadewijch of Brabant in Old Dutch, of which language I know nothing: it was pure music. It might have been a very beautiful string quartet.

27. Though in Gerard Manley Hopkins features of sound, especially stress and rhythm, can seem to do nearly all the work of meaning on their own.

28. Though again the point holds, obviously, for pure music, not for song, not for opera.

29. See chapter 8, the section "Whose Reality?"

30. Terry Eagleton wrote a wonderful little book decades ago called *The Body as Language* (London: Sheed and Ward, 1970), no doubt long out of print, and I am deeply indebted to it.

31. *The Birth of Tragedy*, ed. Raymond Geuss and Ronald Speirs, trans. Ronald Speirs (Cambridge: Cambridge University Press, 2000), 37.

32. Férdia Stone-Davis objects that the cat is not entirely absent from music, whether as "subject" or as "object." There is a gap between the music as written score and the actual performance of it by the players on the one side; and there is likewise a gap between the performance and its reception by a hearer on the other side, and these gaps are filled by the individualities of the performers and listeners. At those two points, she says, the cat comes back into it. And this is true, though it is not clear to me that anything in what I say about music here entails the denial of it; for it remains the case that even if Beethoven's *Eroica* symphony exists only as performed, and thus as performed and heard by individuals, the *Eroica* retains its identity as Beethoven's E flat symphony independently of particular performances:

for the E flat symphony is what those performances are performances *of.* And even as to those performances, it is true of each of them that "what you hear is what you get." The players and the hearers still do not come into its character as music in the way that Beatrice comes into her smile to Dante, where its being *Beatrice's* smile is intrinsic to the smile's identity and meaning.

33. In his antiphon for Vespers on the feast of Corpus Christi.

34. That is, if it is any good. Much music neither says nor does anything at all.

35. If it is a *futurae gloriae nobis pignus,* "a pledge of future glory," it is also a *memoria passionis eius,* "a remembrance of his passion."

36. This distinction between reason in its maximal and minimal senses corresponds pretty accurately with Augustine's distinction respectively between *ratio superior* and *ratio inferior:* see *De Trinitate* 12.1.

37. *ST* 1a, q. 12, art. 13, ad. 1.

FOUR.   Metaphor, Poetry, and Allegory

1. For the Latin text, see Thomas Aquinas, *Quaestiones quodlibetales* [hereafter *Quodlibet*], ed. Raimundi Spiazzi (Rome: Marietti, 1949). For an English translation, see Denys Turner, *Eros and Allegory, Medieval Exegesis of the Song of Songs* (Kalamazoo, MI: Cistercian Publications, 1995), 343–58.

2. James A. Weisheipl, *Friar Thomas D'Aquino, His Life, Thought and Works* (Oxford: Blackwell, 1975), 105–7.

3. Ibid. Nearly all recent scholarship dates *Quodlibet* 7 to Thomas's first regency in Paris and to either 1256 or 1257. Jean-Pierre Torrell, in his *Saint Thomas Aquinas,* vol. 1, *The Person and His Work,* trans. Robert Royal (Washington, DC: Catholic University of America Press, 1996), says nothing to contradict, nor anything to support, Weisheipl's contention that this *Quodlibet* is in truth a Disputed Question conducted by Thomas at his inception.

4. Thomas Aquinas, *Summa theologiae* [hereafter *ST*] 1a, q. 1, arts. 9–10.

5. In the parallel discussion in the *Summa theologiae* Thomas raises the question of whether *sacra doctrina* may properly be described as *argumentativa,* to which, of course, he replies that it must.

6. See *Quodlibet* 7, q. 6, art. 1, obj. 2.

7. *Quodlibet* 7, q. 6, art. 1, ad. 4.

8. *Quodlibet* 7, q. 6, art. 1, obj. 4, and *ST* 1a, q.1, art. 10, ad. 1.

9. *Quodlibet* 7, q. 6, art. 2, ad. 1.

10. *Quodlibet* 7, q. 6, art. 1, ad. 1.

11. *Quodlibet* 7, q. 6, art. 3, obj. 2.

12. *Quodlibet* 7, q. 6, art. 2, corp.

13. *Quodlibet* 7, q. 6, art. 1, corp.

14. For a partial translation, see Turner, *Eros and Allegory,* 383–90.

15. See ibid., 394.

16. *Secundum Salomonem: A Thirteenth Century Latin Commentary on the Song of Solomon*, ed. S. Kamin and A. Saltman (Ramat Gan: Bar Ilan University Press, 1989).

17. Rashi pursues the historical significance of the text right up to his own times, and so reads the significance of the Shulamite woman's vicissitudes as metaphors for, among other historical events, the Christian persecutions of the Jewish people. For obvious reasons the Christian author of the *Expositio hystorica* cuts the historical reference back to pre-Christian times.

18. *Expositio hystorica* 1.9–16.

19. Kamin and Saltman, introduction to *Secundum Salomonem*, 12.

20. *Sermon* 9.7, in Bernard of Clairvaux, *On the Song of Songs*, vol. 1, trans. Kilian Walsh, O. C. S. O. (Kalamazoo, MI: Cistercian Publications, 1977), 58–59.

21. *Sermon* 3.1, trans. Walsh, 16.

22. *Sermon* 1.8, trans. Walsh, 5.

23. *Sermon* 1.11, trans. Walsh, 6–7.

24. *Sermon* 7.2, trans. Walsh, 39.

25. *Sermon* 1.5, trans. Walsh, 3–4.

26. Denys the Carthusian, *Enarratio in Canticum Canticorum* [hereafter *In Cant.*], art. 2, in *In Proverbia, Ecclesiasten, Canticum Canticorum, Sapientiam*, ed. M. Leone, Doctoris ecstatici D. Dionysii Cartusiensis opera omnia 7 (Montreuil: Typis Cartusiae S. M. de Pratis, 1898), 296B, trans. Turner, *Eros and Allegory*, 420.

27. *In Cant.*, art. 2, ed. Leone, 296A'–B', trans. Turner, *Eros and Allegory*, 421.

28. *In Cant.*, prol., ed. Leone, 292, trans. Turner, *Eros and Allegory*, 415.

29. The gender is important here. Not considered in this essay is the genre of late medieval spiritually erotic poetry in the vernacular, almost entirely authored by women, Gertrude the Great of Helfta, Hadewijch of Brabant, and others, in whom the eroticism is direct, unapologetic, and enthusiastic, not mediated by allegory, and for one very obvious reason (among many others): the women do not have to invert their genders in order to identify with the Bride, as do the men. Bernard is an enthusiastic woman; Denys an unrepentantly pedantic man.

30. Most influentially by Origen (see *On First Principles*, chap. 4, trans. Rowan A. Greer, *Origen* [New York: Paulist Press, 1979], 187–88) and by Gregory the Great (see my translation of the brief torso of his commentary on the Song in *Eros and Allegory*, 215–55).

31. John of the Cross, *Spiritual Canticle*, prol., trans. K. Kavanaugh and O. Rodriguez (Washington, DC: Institute of Carmelite Studies Publications, 1991), 469–70.

32. Origen, *On First Principles*, trans. Greer, 187–88.

33. Willis Barnstone, *The Poems of St. John of the Cross* (Bloomington: Indiana University Press, 1968), 30.

34. Ibid.

35. See Robert Graves's introduction to *The Poems of St. John of the Cross*, revised English versions by John Frederick Nims (New York: Grove Press, 1968).

36. My translation. For a complete translation of the *Spiritual Canticle*, see my *Eros and Allegory*, 207–14.

37. Quoted in Roy Campbell, preface to *The Poems of St. John of the Cross*, ed. M. D'Arcy, S.J. (London: Harvill, 1952), 1.

FIVE. Why Was Marguerite Porete Burned?

1. Guy II was bishop of Cambrai from 1296 to 1306, so Marguerite's first condemnation must have taken place between those years. We have no exact date for the composition of the text of the *Mirror* itself, except that in some form or other it predates 1306, and since it comes to the attention of Guy, as Babinsky says, it presumably circulated in some number of copies, publicly, therefore, and not merely privately, so that in any case she would not have been in a position to suppress them all. See Marguerite Porete, *The Mirror of Simple Souls*, trans. and introd. Ellen Babinsky (New York: Paulist Press, 1993), 26. Otherwise the addendum of a postscript (chap. 140) adverting to the more or less enthusiastic approval of her work by three theologians, the Franciscan John of Querayn, a Cistercian, Frank Cantor, and a Parisian master, Godfrey of Fontaines, obviously must postdate the original composition of her text.

2. O my lover, what will beguines say
   and religious types
   When they hear the excellence
   of your divine song?
   Beguines I say err. . . .
   (Porete, *Mirror*, chap. 122, trans. Babinsky, 200)

If Marguerite had ever been a Beguine it would have been as a mendicant and uncloistered follower of its spirituality, not, as were the majority, living in community with other women and following a rule of common life. See Bernard McGinn, *The Flowering of Mysticism: Men and Women in the New Mysticism*, vol. 3 of *The Presence of God: A History of Western Christian Mysticism* (New York: Crossroad, 1998), 244.

3. See Oliver Davies, *Meister Eckhart, Mystical Theologian* (London: SPCK, 1992), 22–45, for an excellent short discussion of the complex relations between the condemnations of Marguerite Porete and Meister Eckhart.

4. Though Jean Gerson very probably would have; see chapter 6 below.

5. Marguerite Porete, *Speculum simplicium animarum; Le mirouer des simples âmes* 140.1–33, though the French text of this chapter is missing from the only available MS and is supplied in the Middle English and Latin translations in the

edition prepared by Romana Guarnieri and Paul Verdeyen for Corpus Christianorum Continuatio Medievalis 69 (Turnhout: Brepols, 1986). Throughout I have
used the CCCM edition, making my own translations.

6. Robert E. Lerner, *The Heresy of the Free Spirit in the Later Middle Ages*
(Berkeley: University of California Press, 1972), 74.

7. Ibid.

8. As late as 1928 a modern English translation of the Old French text was
published in London with the imprimatur of the cardinal archbishop of Westmin-
ster, the original being attributed to "an anonymous Carthusian of the fourteenth
century." It was not until 1946 that the editors of the CCCM text reconnected it
with the work for which Marguerite was condemned in 1310.

9. Apart from the earlier studies of Lerner and Lambert, notable studies in
English include a collection of papers, *Meister Eckhart and the Beguine Mystics*,
ed. Bernard McGinn (New York: Continuum, 1994); McGinn's *Flowering of Mysticism*, 3:244–265; Ellen Babinsky's introduction and notes to her English translation of Porete's *Mirror*; Michael Sells in *Mystical Languages of Unsaying* (Chicago:
University of Chicago Press, 1994); and most recently, *A Companion to Marguerite
Porete and the Mirror of Simple Souls* (Leiden: Brill, 2017).

10. For extracts from Eckhart's defense and the bull *In agro Dominico* of
1329, see Meister Eckhart, *The Essential Sermons, Commentaries, Treatises and Defense*, trans. E. Colledge and B. McGinn (London: SPCK, 1981), 71–81.

11. McGinn, *Flowering of Mysticism*, 251.

12. The "unencumbered soul," as she calls it, the soul that wills nothing for
herself, "has her right name from the nothingness in which she rests. And since
she is nothing, she is concerned about nothing, neither about herself, nor about
her neighbors, nor even about God himself. For she is so small that she cannot be
found, and every created thing is so far from her that she cannot feel it. And God
is so great that she can comprehend nothing of him. On account of such nothingness she has fallen into certainty of knowing nothing and into certainty of willing
nothing" (*Mirror*, chap. 81, trans. Babinsky, 156).

13. M. Lambert, *Medieval Heresy*, 2nd ed. (Oxford: Blackwell, 1992).

14. Otto Langer, *Mystische Erfahrung und Spirituelle Theologie* (Munich:
Artemis, 1987), 18–20; Davies, *Meister Eckhart*, 72–75.

15. The phrase "negation of the negation" as such is anachronistic, being
Eckhart's own. It is not used by Marguerite. To note Marguerite's austerity of imagery is not to deny that she uses the imagery of courtly and erotic love. She does
use it extensively and with an exuberance that matches that of Mechtild of Magde-
burg. See *Mirror*, chap. 1. What characterizes Marguerite's vocabulary and places
her firmly within the mainstream tradition of negative theology is the apophatic
control that she exercises over the exuberance of her affirmative vocabulary.

16. I owe the "flirtatious playfulness" characterization of Marguerite's rhetorical and theological style, and much more of substance, to Rebecca Stephens.

17. Porete, *Mirror*, trans. Babinsky, 117.

18. Ibid., 97.

19. Ibid., 30.

20. Ibid., 133.

21. Lerner, *Heresy*, 83.

22. Lambert, *Medieval Heresy*, 187.

23. Lerner, *Heresy*, 68.

24. Davies, *Meister Eckhart*, 37.

25. Ibid., 39.

26. K. Ruh, *Meister Eckhart: Theologe, Prediger, Mystiker* (Munich: Beck, 1985), 107.

27. Davies, *Meister Eckhart*, 67.

28. Petrus de Estate and subsequently Albert of Milan, both Franciscans, were among the commissioners appointed by Henry of Virneberg to examine Eckhart's work in Cologne in 1326.

29. Lambert, *Medieval Heresy*, xi.

30. Meister Eckhart, *Defense*, trans. Colledge and McGinn, *Essential Sermons*, 74.

31. Ibid., 76.

32. Ibid., 72. Eckhart, writing in 1326, is referring to the fact that but three years earlier Thomas, some central propositions of whose theology had been condemned by the bishop of Paris, Stephen Tempier, in 1277, was canonized by Pope John XXII.

33. Porete, *Speculum* 43.10–14.

34. Porete, *Speculum* 13.31–40.

35. Porete, *Speculum* 13.51–67.

36. Porete, *Speculum* 13.46–50.

37. Porete, *Speculum* 6.1–7, 26.

38. Porete, *Speculum* 8.1–8.

39. Porete, *Speculum* 8.9–14.

40. Porete, *Speculum* 7.27–33.

41. William of St. Thierry, *The Golden Epistle* 1.42, trans. Theodore Berkeley (Kalamazoo, MI: Cistercian Publications), 67; Peter Lombard, *Sentences* 1, d. 17. Bernard McGinn, however, says that Marguerite Porete takes a step theologically beyond William's "by following this statement with an apophatic paradox undercutting any stable description of such union: 'This union place the Soul in the being without being that is being.'" McGinn, *Flowering of Mysticism*, 262.

42. William of St. Thierry, *Golden Epistle*, 1.42.169–70, trans. Berkeley, 67.

43. Porete, *Speculum* 21.44–45.

44. William of St. Thierry, *Golden Epistle* 2.16, trans. Berkeley, 263; Porete, *Speculum* 21.46–47.

45. The Holy Spirit warns that the soul "does not possess this [annihilated condition] through divine nature, for this cannot possibly be, but through the power of love, as it ought to be"; Porete, *Speculum* 42.7–9. See also "one will, one love, one work in two natures," Porete, *Speculum* 115.25–26.

46. Porete, *Mirror,* trans. Babinsky, 121; William of St. Thierry, *Golden Epistle* 2.20.276.

47. Thomas Aquinas, *Summa theologiae* [hereafter *ST*] 2-2ae, q. 23, art. 2.

48. *ST* 2-2ae, q. 23, art. 2, corp.

49. *ST* 2-2ae, q. 23, a. 2, ad. 1.

50. Of the three known articles of condemnation of Marguerite's opinions (April 11, 1310), the first reads: "Quod anima adnichilata dat licentiam virtutibus nec est amplius in earum servitute, quia non habet eas quoad usum sed virtutes obediunt ad nutum" ([She holds] that the annihilated soul sets the virtues free and is no longer in bondage to them, for she no longer possesses them as to their use, but obeys them in their true sense). McGinn, *Flowering of Mysticism,* 437n243.

51. Porete, *Speculum* 8.9–13, and 21.7–31.

52. McGinn, *Flowering of Mysticism,* 251.

six.   The "Uniting Wisdom of Love"

1. "Vir mirabilis atque divinitus unctus magnifice et eruditus, Joannes Ruysbroeck." Denys the Carthusian, *De contemplatione* 2.9B', in *Opera minora,* vol. 9, ed. M. Leone, Doctoris ecstatici D. Dionysii Carthusiensis, Opera Omnia 41 (Tournai: Typis Cartusiae S. M. de Pratis, 1912), 247.

2. For a more extended account, see Bernard McGinn, *The Varieties of Vernacular Mysticism,* vol. 5 of *The Presence of God: A History of Western Christian Mysticism* (New York: Crossroad, 1998), 77–86.

3. In Jean Gerson, *Oeuvres completes,* ed. P. Glorieux, vol. 7, *L'oeuvre spirituelle et pastorelle* (Paris: Desclee, 1968), 615–35, 791–804.

4. Ruusbroec wrote his *Little Book of Clarification* at the request of the Carthusian Brother Gerard, who was anxious about the orthodoxy of some of his earlier writing.

5. In 1446 Denys was subjected to some sort of inquiry by his superiors into what they judged to be his excessively intellectual and scholarly pursuits, on the occasion of which Denys composed a short *Protestatio ad superiorem suum,* in *Opera minora,* 9:625–26.

6. Gerson most probably read Ruusbroec in the Latin translation of Geert Groote, from whose text I have translated Gerson's quotations. All other quotations of Ruusbroec are from Jan van Ruusbroec, *The Spiritual Espousals and Other Works,* ed. James A. Wiseman (New York: Paulist Press, 1985).

7. Gerson, *Oeuvres completes,* ed. Glorieux, 7:615–16.

8. Ibid., 616.

9. Ibid., 617–18.

10. Ibid., 618.

11. Ibid., 627–28; see *Letter 2*, 802, but also 796, where Gerson links Ruusbroec's views with those of the earlier heretic Amaury de Bene.

12. Norman P. Tanner, ed., *Decrees of the Ecumenical Councils*, vol. 1, *Nicaea 1–Lateran V* (London: Sheed and Ward, 1990), 383–84.

13. Robert E. Lerner, *The Heresy of the Free Spirit in the Late Middle Ages* (Notre Dame, IN: University of Notre Dame Press, 1972); Malcolm Lambert, *Medieval Heresy*, 2nd ed. (Oxford: Blackwell, 1992).

14. Lambert, *Medieval Heresy*, 187.

15. Marguerite Porete, *Speculum simplicium animarum; Le mirouer des simples âmes*, ed. Romana Guarnieri and Paul Verdeyen, Corpus Christianorum Continuatio Medievalis 69 (Turnhout: Brepols, 1986).

16. These descriptions of Marguerite are those of the so-called Continuator of Nangis, who chronicled her trial from a point of view favorable to the inquisitors.

17. Though see Lerner, *Heresy*, 165–66, for Gerson's reference to a heretical "Maria of Valenciennes" commonly identified as Marguerite.

18. For a discussion of the controversies in the period 1330–36 on the issue of the beatific vision, see Simon Tugwell, *Human Immortality and the Redemption of Death* (London: Darton, Longman and Todd, 1990), 133–48.

19. Gerson, *Oeuvres complètes*, ed. Glorieux, 628. The issue here concerns the views of Pope John XXII and others, including Guiral Ot, the Franciscan minister general, who held that the souls of the dead do not enter immediately into the beatific vision but only after the general judgment and final resurrection. Hence, on this view, there is only one "act" of enjoying the beatific vision. The Parisian theologians assembled in 1333 insisted on the orthodoxy of the traditional Latin view, maintained by Thomas Aquinas, that these souls enjoy the beatific vision after their particular judgment and before the general judgment but that after the general judgment they enjoy it more fully. Hence, their beatitude consists in two acts. It is not entirely clear what led Gerson to connect, or confuse, the Vienne condemnation of the Beghards and Beguines with the Parisian decretal on the issue of beatific vision, unless it was that *Ad nostrum* appears to connect the "autotheism" of the Beghards and Beguines with the view that the perfected soul can achieve the beatific vision fully in this life (see Tanner, *Decrees*, 383), though of course both sides in the controversies of the 1330s would have accepted the condemnation of that view.

20. Gerson, *Oeuvres complètes*, ed. Glorieux, 618–19.

21. Bernard of Clairvaux, *De diligendo Deo*, 10.28: "Sic affici, deificari est. Quomodo stilla acquae modica multo infusa vino, deficere se tota videtur, dum et saporem induit et colorem."

22. Gerson, *Oeuvres complètes*, ed. Glorieux, 620.

23. Ibid.

24. Ibid., 620–21.

25. Ibid., 621.

26. Ibid., 618–19.

27. Ibid., 624.

28. See Wiseman's commentary in Ruusbroec, *Spiritual Espousals*, 251–52.

29. Denys the Carthusian, *De contemplatione* 3.25, in *Opera minora*, vol. 9, ed. Leone, 288C–D.

30. Ibid., 288D–A', 288A'.

31. Ibid., 288B'–C'.

32. Ibid., 288C'–D'.

33. Gerson, *Oeuvres complètes*, ed. Glorieux, 629–30: "Ad talium . . . quaestionum determinationem . . . non sufficit quod homo sit devotus."

34. Peter Lombard, *Sentences*, I, d.17, 1, 1: "Cum ergo de dilectione diligimus fratrem de Deo diligimus fratrem." For William of St. Thierry, see *Golden Epistle* 1.169, trans. Theodore Berkeley, O. C. S. O., in *The Works of William of St. Thierry*, Cistercian Fathers Series 12 (Kalamazoo, MI: Cistercian Publications, 1980), 67.

35. Augustine, *De Trinitate* 15.17.

36. Thomas Aquinas, *Summa theologiae* [hereafter *ST*] 2-2ae, q. 23, art. 2, obj. 1.

37. *ST* 2-2ae, q. 23, art. 2, ad. 1.

38. Emily Brontë, *Wuthering Heights*, chap. 9.

39. Augustine, *Confessions* 3.6: "Tu autem eras interius intimo meo."

40. Brontë, *Wuthering Heights*, chap. 9.

41. "The Extasie," in *John Donne, A Selection of His Poetry*, ed. John Hayward (Harmondsworth: Penguin Books, 1969), 56–57.

42. Brontë, *Wuthering Heights*, chap. 9.

43. *Purgation and Purgatory*, in Catherine of Genoa, *Purgation and Purgatory, The Spiritual Dialogue*, trans. Serge Hughes, Classics of Western Spirituality (New York: Paulist Press, 1979), 80.

44. Ruusbroec, *Spiritual Espousals* 3, ed. Wiseman, 149.

45. For example, "I have . . . said that no creature can become or be so holy that it loses its creatureliness and becomes God." Jan van Ruusbroec, *Little Book of Clarification*, in *Spiritual Espousals*, ed. Wiseman, 252.

SEVEN.   Why Is There Anything?

1. See Natarajan's *Mapping the Heavens: The Radical Scientific Ideas That Reveal the Cosmos* (New Haven, CT: Yale University Press, 2016).

2. Richard Dawkins, *The God Delusion* (Boston: Mariner Books, 2006); Daniel Dennett, *Darwin's Dangerous Idea, Evolution and the Meanings of Life* (New York: Simon and Schuster, 1995).

3. Della Rocca is the Andrew Downey Orrick Professor of Philosophy at Yale University.

4. Here we need another clarification, lest it be supposed that as a Christian I am called upon to answer the question what it's all for as if there were some purpose you need to know about that God had in mind in creating the universe. This is indeed a view that some Christians have, namely that the created universe is a sort of instrument in God's hand serving for some divine purpose beyond it. For myself I am rather of the view that we have a world, any sort of world, not because God has some purpose he needed served by its creation but because God just fancied the idea of it, its existence being the outcome of an explosion of delight in his creativity: more as an artist does than as engineers do. As Thomas Aquinas says, God does nothing *secundum utilitatem suam,* for God has no unmet desires that need serving; he acts only because he is infinitely good and acts on no other terms (See *Summa theologiae* 1a, q. 44, ad. 1). But that sort of statement famously presents problems, especially those associated with the existence of evil in the world that, de facto, we have. That, though, is another story.

5. Aristotle, *Physics* 219a.30.

6. Augustine, *Confessions* 11.12–13.

7. A reading of the book of Genesis that is of course itself disputable and disputed.

EIGHT.   The Price of Truth

1. In Herbert McCabe, *God Matters* (London: Geoffrey Chapman, 1987), 249.

2. I wish it were not necessary to explain that in speaking in this way of how the Eucharist effects a change in the meaning of bread I do not deny that there is a change in reality, an ontological change, so that the bread and wine truly become the body and blood of Christ, and not just "for us" and merely symbolically. There are Roman Catholics who simply do not know their own sacramental theology, and I will not feel held to account by those who would set the ontology of the sacraments at odds with the epistemology. It is a Zwinglian instinct, not a Catholic, that imagines the character of the Eucharist as sign must be set at odds with the reality of eucharistic change, and it is a bad Catholic instinct, condemned at Trent, that would prioritize either so as to diminish the other. The properly Catholic position is, as Thomas Aquinas says, that a sacrament is a "sacred sign that effects what it signifies": its efficacy and its sign value are inseparable.

3. John 15:18–27.

4. Somewhere in *Capital,* vol. 1. I can't seem to find it.

5. Thomas Aquinas, *Summa Theologiae* 1a, q. 44, art. 4, ad. 1.

INDEX

D E N Y S   T U R N E R

is Horace Tracy Pitkin Professor Emeritus at Yale University, and a lecturer in religion at Princeton University.

Printed in the USA
CPSIA information can be obtained
at www.ICGtesting.com
LVHW042131191023
761249LV00032B/66